SAM SHEPARD

TRUE WEST

W0296018

Cornelsen

Sam Shepard
True West

Herausgegeben von:
Arthur Kutsch

Verlagsredaktion: Neil Porter

Technische Umsetzung: Ingo Ostermaier

Umschlagillustrationen:
Großes Bild: © zefa/masterfile/Daryl Benson
Kleines Bild: Fotofinder © dia/mediacolors

Copyright © 1980, Sam Shepard

www.cornelsen.de

1. Auflage, 6. Druck 2008 / 06

Alle Drucke dieser Auflage sind inhaltlich unverändert und können im Unterricht nebeneinander verwendet werden.

© 2005 Cornelsen Verlag, Berlin

Das Werk und seine Teile sind urheberrechtlich geschützt.
Jede Nutzung in anderen als den gesetzlich zugelassenen Fällen bedarf der vorherigen schriftlichen Einwilligung des Verlages.
Hinweis zu § 52 a UrhG: Weder das Werk noch seine Teile dürfen ohne eine solche Einwilligung eingescannt und in ein Netzwerk eingestellt werden.
Dies gilt auch für Intranets von Schulen und sonstigen Bildungseinrichtungen.

Druck: CS-Druck CornelsenStürtz, Berlin

ISBN 978-3-06-031186-6

Inhalt gedruckt auf säurefreiem Papier aus nachhaltiger Forstwirtschaft.

CONTENTS

Colloquial American English

In *True West* the characters use the idiom of colloquial American, i.e. a lower level of spoken American English. Thus the spelling reflects the pronunciation of the words as used by the characters. As Lee is not well-educated, his speech contains many informal American pronunciations that may at first make the play a little difficult to read. Before you start reading it would be a good idea to look at the following typical speech patterns that you will find in the play.

Letters/syllables substituted by an apostrophe:

– at the beginning of words:

'at's	that's (p. 12, l. 7)	*'course*	of course (p. 31, l. 4)
'd	did (p. 13, l. 15)	*'til*	until (p. 50, l. 2)
'em	them (p. 22, l. 15)	*'fraid*	afraid (p. 52, l. 20)
'cause	because (p. 30, l. 8)	*'n*	than (p. 62, l. 5)
'bout	about (p. 30, l. 13)		

– at the end of words:

a'	of (p. 12, l.2)	*sorta'*	sort of (p. 11, l. 10)
		kinda'	kind of (p. 11, l. 21)
		lota'	a lot of (p. 13, l. 4)
		outa'	out of (p. 22, l. 2)
		lotsa'	lots of (p. 42, l. 18)
		fulla'	full of (p. 45, l. 10)
		a' course	of course (p. 49, l. 11)
–in'	–ing	*keepin'*	keeping (p. 11, l. 15)
		botherin'	bothering (p. 13, l. 1)
		nothin'	nothing (p. 13, l. 2)
		doin'	doing (p. 13, l. 10)
		gettin'	getting (p. 20, l. 15)
a'	have	*musta'*	must have (p. 33, l. 17)
		shouldn't a'	should not have (p. 34, l. 14)
		shoulda' seen	should have seen (p. 48, l. 10)
		oughta'	ought to (p. 49, l. 6)
offa'		off a (p. 19, l. 13); off of = off (p. 40, l. 4)	

Contractions

gimme	give me (p. 25, l. 2)	*lemme*	let me (p. 84, l. 13)
helluva'	hell of a (p. 20, l. 18)	*dunno'*	don't know (p. 67, l. 19)
gotta'	(have) got to (p. 15, l. 5)	*wanna*	want to (p. 13, l. 1)
gonna	going to (p. 11, l. 19)	*dya'*	do you (p. 83, l. 5)
whadya'	what do you (p. 24, l. 11)	*what d'ya*	what do you (p. 14, l. 1)
what'sa'	what's the (p. 15, l. 9)	*what's he*	what has he (p. 24, l. 5)

Pronunciation

fer	for (p. 16, l. 5)	*jest*	just (p. 49, l. 23)
git	get (p. 15, l. 17)	*forgit*	forget (p. 17, l. 17)
naw	no (p. 12, l. 9)	*yeah*	yes (p. 11, l. 9)
ya'	you (p. 11, l. 16)	*yer*	your (p. 13, l. 1), you are (p. 13, l. 10)

Non-standard grammar

he/she don't	he/she doesn't (p. 11, l. 15)
that don't	that doesn't (p. 33, l. 14)
don't it	doesn't it (p. 42, l. 13)
he wouldn't a' gave	he wouldn't have given (p. 47, l. 4)
I seen him	I saw him (p. 13, l. 20)
I been	I've been (p. 17, l. 15)
I ever saw	I have ever seen (p. 71, ll. 4–5)
I didn't do nothin'	I didn't do anything (p. 51, l. 21)
you don't have to say nothin'	you don't have to say anything (p. 14, l. 7)
ya' got / ya' got?	you have got (p. 12, l. 2), have you got? (p. 12, l. 3)
you going to …?	are you going to (p. 14, l. 11)

Abbreviations and Annotations

adj	adjective	infml	informal
adv	adverb	jdm./jdn.	jemandem/en
AE	American English	n	noun
cf.	confer; see	p., pp.	page, pages
derog	derogatory	pl	plural
e.g.	exempli gratia; for example	sb.	somebody
esp.	especially	sl	slang
etc.	et cetera; and so on	sth.	something
fml	formal	usu.	usually
i.e.	id est; in other words	v	verb

The annotations are arranged chronologically: the first time a word is used is where you will find it explained. All pronunciations given are American English. An alphabetical list of all the annotated words can be found at **www.learnetix.de/bookshelf**.

TRUE WEST

Characters:

Austin: Early thirties, light blue sports shirt, light tan cardigan sweater, clean blue jeans, white tennis shoes

Lee: His older brother, early forties, filthy white T-shirt, tattered brown overcoat covered with dust, dark blue baggy suit pants from the Salvation Army, pink suede belt, pointed black forties' dress shoes scuffed up, holes in the soles, no socks, no hat, long pronounced sideburns, 'Gene Vincent' hairdo, two days' growth of beard, bad teeth

Saul Kimmer: Late forties, Hollywood producer, pink and white flower-print sports shirt, white sports coat with matching polyester slacks, black and white loafers

Mom: Early sixties, mother of the brothers, small woman, conservative white skirt and matching jacket, red shoulder bag, two pieces of matching red luggage

True West was first performed at the Magic Theatre in San Francisco on July 10, 1980.

▷ **2** *tan:* light yellowish brown • *cardigan:* woollen jacket fastened with buttons **4** *filthy:* very dirty • *tattered:* old and torn **5** *baggy:* loose-fitting • *pants* (pl; AE): trousers **6** *suede belt* [sweɪd]: Wildledergürtel **6–7** *dress shoes:* elegant shoes; evening shoes **7** *scuffed up:* damaged **7–8** *pronounced:* very noticeable **8** *sideburns* (pl): Koteletten • *Gene Vincent* (born 1935): rock and roll singer in the early 1960s • *hairdo:* hairstyle **11** *matching* (adj): having the same color, pattern, etc. as sth. else so that they look good together **12** *slacks* (pl; AE): casual trousers • *loafers* (pl): flat leather shoes for casual or sports wear **16** *Magic Theatre:* theater founded in 1967 which only produces new plays

Scene:

All nine scenes take place on the same set; a kitchen and adjoining alcove of an older home in a Southern California suburb, about forty miles east of L.A. The kitchen takes up the majority of the playing area to stage left (from the actor's point of view, facing the audience). The kitchen consists of a sink, upstage center, surrounded by counter space, a wall telephone, cupboards and a small window just above it bordered by neat yellow curtains. Stage left of sink is a stove. Stage right, a refrigerator. The alcove adjoins the kitchen to stage right. There is no wall division or door to the alcove. It is open and easily accessible from the kitchen and defined only by the objects in it: a small, round, glass breakfast table mounted on white iron legs; two matching white iron chairs set across from each other. The two exterior walls of the alcove which prescribe a corner in the upstage right are composed of many small windows beginning from a solid wall about three feet high and extending to the ceiling. The windows look out to bushes and citrus trees. The alcove is filled with all sorts of house plants in various pots, mostly Boston ferns hanging in planters at different levels. The floor of the alcove is composed of green synthetic grass.

All entrances and exits are made stage left from the kitchen. There is no door. The actors simply go off and come onto the playing area.

Note on set and costume:

The set should be constructed realistically with no attempt to distort its dimensions, shapes, objects or colors. No objects should be introduced which might draw special attention to themselves other than the props demanded by the script. If a stylistic "concept" is grafted onto the set design it will only serve to confuse the evolution of the characters' situation, which is the most important focus of the play.

▷ **3** *alcove:* Nische, Nebenraum **6** *sink:* Spülbecken **6–7** *counter space:* working area (*counter:* Arbeitsplatte) **11** *accessible:* easy to reach **14** *prescribe:* (here) form **18** *Boston fern:* popular fern (= Farn) grown as a potted houseplant **19** *planter:* container in which plants are grown **24** *distort sth.:* change sth. so that it loses its form **27** *prop:* object that is required on a stage **27–28** *be grafted onto sth.:* (here) be added to sth.

Likewise, the costumes should be exactly representative of who the characters are, and not added onto for the sake of making a point to the audience.

NOTE ON SOUND:

The Coyote of southern California has a distinct yapping, dog-like bark, similar to a Hyena. This yapping grows more intense and maniacal as the pack grows in numbers, which is usually the case when they lure and kill pets from suburban yards. The sense of growing frenzy in the pack should be felt in the background, particularly in Scenes Seven and Eight. In any case, these Coyotes never make the long, mournful, solitary howl of the Hollywood stereotype.

The sound of Crickets can speak for itself.

These sounds should also be treated realistically even though they sometimes grow in volume and numbers.

▷ **5** *yap* (v): bark making a high sharp sound **6** *hyena* [haɪ'iːnə]: Hyäne **7** *maniacal* [mə'naɪekl]: sounding as if you are crazy • *pack:* group of dogs **8** *lure sb./sth.* [lʊr]: attract sb./sth. **9** *frenzy:* hysteria; wild excitement **12** *cricket:* Grille

ACT ONE

SCENE ONE

Night, sound of crickets in dark, candlelight appears in alcove illuminating AUSTIN *seated at glass table, hunched over a writing notebook, pen in hand, cigarette burning in ashtray, cup of coffee, typewriter on table, stacks of paper, candle burning on table. Soft moonlight fills kitchen, illuminating* LEE, *beer in hand, six-pack on counter behind him, he's leaning against sink, mildly drunk, takes slug of beer.*

LEE: So, Mom took off for Alaska, huh?

AUSTIN: Yeah.

LEE: Sorta' left you in charge.

AUSTIN: Well, she knew I was coming down here so she offered me the place.

LEE: You keepin' the plants watered?

AUSTIN: Yeah.

LEE: Keepin' the sink clean? She don't like even a single tea leaf in the sink ya' know.

AUSTIN: [*Trying to concentrate on writing*] Yeah, I know.

[*Pause*]

LEE: She gonna' be up there a long time?

AUSTIN: I don't know.

LEE: Kinda' nice for you, huh? Whole place to yourself.

▷ **2** *hunch over:* bend the upper part of your body over sth. **4** *stack* (n): heap, pile **7** *(a) slug of* (AE infml): a mouthful of (an alcoholic drink) **8** *take off for* (infml): leave a place for (another place) **10** *in charge:* responsible for sth., in control of sth.

AUSTIN: Yeah, it's great.

LEE: Ya' got crickets anyway. Tons a' crickets out there. [*Looks around kitchen*] Ya' got groceries? Coffee?

AUSTIN: [*Looking up from writing*] What?

LEE: You got coffee?

AUSTIN: Yeah.

LEE: 'At's good. [*Short pause.*] Real coffee? From the bean?

AUSTIN: Yeah. You want some?

LEE: Naw. I brought some uh – [*Motions to beer.*]

AUSTIN: Help yourself to whatever's – [*Motions to refrigerator.*]

LEE: I will. Don't worry about me. I'm not the one to worry about. I mean I can uh – [*Pause.*] You always work by candlelight?

AUSTIN: No – uh – Not always.

LEE: Just sometimes?

AUSTIN: [*Puts pen down, rubs his eyes*] Yeah. Sometimes it's soothing.

LEE: Isn't that what the old guys did?

AUSTIN: What old guys?

LEE: The Forefathers. You know.

AUSTIN: Forefathers?

LEE: Isn't that what they did? Candlelight burning into the night? Cabins in the wilderness.

AUSTIN: [*Rubs hand through his hair*] I suppose.

▷ **9** *motion to sth.:* point to sth. **16** *soothing* (adj): relaxing, comforting **17** *guy* (infml): man

LEE: I'm not botherin' you am I? I mean I don't wanna break into yer uh – concentration or nothin'.

AUSTIN: No, it's all right.

LEE: That's good. I mean I realize that yer line a' work demands a lota' concentration.

AUSTIN: It's okay.

LEE: You probably think that I'm not fully able to comprehend somethin' like that, huh?

AUSTIN: Like what?

LEE: That stuff yer doin'. That art. You know. Whatever you call it.

AUSTIN: It's just a little research.

LEE: You may not know it but I did a little art myself once.

AUSTIN: You did?

LEE: Yeah! I did some a' that. I fooled around with it. No future in it.

AUSTIN: What'd you do?

LEE: Never mind what I did! Just never mind about that. [*Pause.*] It was ahead of its time.

[*Pause*]

AUSTIN: So, you went out to see the old man, huh?

LEE: Yeah, I seen him.

AUSTIN: How's he doing?

LEE: Same. He's doin' just about the same.

AUSTIN: I was down there too, you know.

▷ **2** *or nothing* (infml): used for emphasis **10** *stuff* (infml): used to refer to things that people do, say, etc. **16** *never mind:* used to tell sb. to not ask about sth.

LEE: What d'ya' want, an award? You want some kinda' medal? You were down there. He told me all about you.

AUSTIN: What'd he say?

LEE: He told me. Don't worry.

[*Pause*]

AUSTIN: Well –

LEE: You don't have to say nothin'.

AUSTIN: I wasn't.

LEE: Yeah, you were gonna' make somethin' up. Somethin' brilliant.

[*Pause*]

AUSTIN: You going to be down here very long, Lee?

LEE: Might be. Depends on a few things.

AUSTIN: You got some friends down here?

LEE: [*Laughs*] I know a few people. Yeah.

AUSTIN: Well, you can stay here as long as I'm here.

LEE: I don't need your permission do I?

AUSTIN: No.

LEE: I mean she's my mother too, right?

AUSTIN: Right.

LEE: She might've just as easily asked me to take care of her place as you.

AUSTIN: That's right.

LEE: I mean I know how to water plants.

▷ **18** *I mean:* used to introduce an explanation for what you have just said

[*Long pause*]

AUSTIN: So you don't know how long you'll be staying then?

LEE: Depends mostly on houses, ya' know.

AUSTIN: Houses?

LEE: Yeah. Houses. Electric devices. Stuff like that. I gotta' make a little tour first.

[*Short pause*]

AUSTIN: Lee, why don't you just try another neighborhood, all right?

LEE: [*Laughs*] What'sa' matter with this neighborhood? This is a great neighborhood. Lush. Good class a' people. Not many dogs.

AUSTIN: Well, our uh – Our mother just happens to live here. That's all.

LEE: Nobody's gonna' know. All they know is somethin's missing. That's all. She'll never even hear about it. Nobody's gonna' know.

AUSTIN: You're going to get picked up if you start walking around here at night.

LEE: Me? I'm gonna' git picked up? What about you? You stick out like a sore thumb. Look at you. You think yer regular lookin'?

AUSTIN: I've got too much to deal with here to be worrying about –

LEE: Yer not gonna' have to worry about me! I've been doin' all right without you. I haven't been anywhere near you for five years! Now isn't that true?

AUSTIN: Yeah.

▷ **5** *devices:* machines, products **10** *lush* (adj): (here) showing wealth and comfort **17** *get picked up* (infml): be arrested (by the police) **17–18** *stick out like a sore thumb* (idiom): be very obvious or noticeable **18** *regular looking* (infml): (here) looking normal and being properly dressed

Lee: So you don't have to worry about me. I'm a free agent.

Austin: All right.

Lee: Now all I wanna' do is borrow yer car.

Austin: No!

Lee: Just fer a day. One day.

Austin: No!

Lee: I won't take it outside a twenty-mile radius. I promise ya'. You can check the speedometer.

Austin: You're not borrowing my car! That's all there is to it.

[*Pause*]

Lee: Then I'll just take the damn thing.

Austin: Lee, look – I don't want any trouble, all right?

Lee: That's a dumb line. That is a dumb fuckin' line. You git paid fer dreamin' up a line like that?

Austin: Look, I can give you some money if you need money.

[Lee *suddenly lunges at* Austin, *grabs him violently by the shirt, and shakes him with tremendous power.*]

Lee: Don't you say that to me! Don't you ever say that to me! [*Just as suddenly* Lee *turns* Austin *loose, pushes him away and backs off.*] You may be able to git away with that with the old man. Git him tanked up for a week! Buy him off with yer Hollywood blood money, but not me! I can git my own money my own way. Big money!

▷ **1** *free agent:* person who is free to make their own decisions **8** *speedometer* [spɪˈdɑːmətər]: instrument that shows the speed of a vehicle **13** *a dumb line* (infml): a stupid thing to say (*dumb* [dʌm]: stupid) **16** *lunge at sb.* [lʌndʒ]: make a sudden movement forward, e.g. in order to attack sb. • *grab sb./sth.:* catch hold of sb./sth., seize sb./sth. **17** *tremendous:* enormous **21** *get sb. tanked up* (infml): make sb. drunk • *buy sb. off:* jdm. bestechen

AUSTIN: I was just making an offer.

LEE: Yeah, well keep it to yourself! [*Long pause.*] Those are the most monotonous fuckin' crickets I ever heard in my life.

AUSTIN: I kinda' like the sound.

LEE: Yeah. Supposed to be able to tell the temperature by the number a' pulses. You believe that?

AUSTIN: The temperature?

LEE: Yeah. The air. How hot it is.

AUSTIN: How do you do that?

LEE: I don't know. Some woman told me that. She was a Botanist. So I believed her.

AUSTIN: Where'd you meet her?

LEE: What?

AUSTIN: The woman Botanist?

LEE: I met her on the desert. I been spendin' a lota' time on the desert.

AUSTIN: What were you doing out there?

LEE: [*Pause, stares in space*] I forgit. Had me a Pit Bull there for a while but I lost him.

AUSTIN: Pit Bull?

LEE: Fightin' dog. Damn, I made some good money off that little dog. Real good money.

[*Pause*]

AUSTIN: You could come up north with me, you know.

LEE: What's up there?

AUSTIN: My family.

▷ **17** *(I) had me a ...*: I had a ... **21** *real* (AE): really

Lee: Oh, that's right, you got the wife and kiddies now don't ya'. The house, the car, the whole slam. That's right.

Austin: You could spend a couple days. See how you like it. I've got an extra room.

Lee: Too cold up there.

[*Pause*]

Austin: You want to sleep for a while?

Lee: [*Pause, stares at* Austin] I don't sleep.

[*Lights to black*]

▷ **1** *kiddie:* young child **2** *the whole slam* (infml): everything

Scene Two

Morning, Austin *is watering plants with a vaporizer,* Lee *sits at glass table in alcove drinking beer.*

Lee: I never realized the old lady was so security-minded.

Austin: How do you mean?

Lee: Made a little tour this morning. She's got locks on everything. Locks and double-locks and chain-locks and – What's she got that's so valuable?

Austin: Antiques I guess. I don't know.

Lee: Antiques! Brought everything with her from the old place, huh. Just the same crap we always had around. Plates and spoons.

Austin: I guess they have personal value to her.

Lee: Personal value. Yeah. Just a lota' junk. Most of it's phony anyway. Idaho decals. Now who in the hell wants to eat offa' plate with the state of Idaho starin' ya' in the face. Every time ya' take a bite ya' get to see a little bit more.

Austin: Well it must mean something to her or she wouldn't save it.

Lee: Yeah, well personally I don't wanna' be invaded by Idaho when I'm eatin'. When I'm eatin' I'm home. Ya' know what I'm sayin'? I'm not driftin', I'm home. I don't need my thoughts swept off to Idaho. I don't need that!

[*Pause*]

Austin: Did you go out last night?

▷ **1** *vaporizer* ['veɪpəraɪzər]: plastic container used to spray plants with water **8** *antiques* [æn'ti:ks]: old and valuable things **10** *crap* (sl): worthless things **12** *junk* (infml): rubbish, useless things of poor quality • *phony* (adj): false or made as an imitation of sth. else **13** *decal* ['di:kæl] (n): Abziehbild **19** *drift:* move from place to place without any aim • *be swept off to sth.:* to be carried away to sth.

LEE: Why?

AUSTIN: I thought I heard you go out.

LEE: Yeah, I went out. What about it?

AUSTIN: Just wondered.

LEE: Damn coyotes kept me awake.

AUSTIN: Oh yeah, I heard them. They must've killed somebody's dog or something.

LEE: Yappin' their fool heads off. They don't yap like that on the desert. They howl. These are city coyotes here.

AUSTIN: Well, you don't sleep anyway do you?

[*Pause*, LEE *stares at him.*]

LEE: You're pretty smart aren't ya'?

AUSTIN: How do you mean?

LEE: I mean you never had any more on the ball than I did. But here you are gettin' invited into prominent people's houses. Sittin' around talkin' like you know somethin'.

AUSTIN: They're not so prominent.

LEE: They're a helluva' lot more prominent than the houses I get invited into.

AUSTIN: Well you invite yourself.

LEE: That's right. I do. In fact I probably got a wider range a' choices than you do, come to think of it.

AUSTIN: I wouldn't doubt it.

▷ **8** *yap your fool head off:* keep on barking loudly for a long time **12** *pretty smart* (infml): rather clever **14** *have sth. on the ball* (infml): be intelligent and capable and clear-thinking **18** *a helluva'* (sl) = *a hell of a:* very much **21** *range:* variety, selection **22** *come to think of it:* when I think about it again/more

LEE: In fact I been inside some pretty classy places in my time. And I never even went to an Ivy League school either.

AUSTIN: You want some breakfast or something?

LEE: Breakfast?

AUSTIN: Yeah. Don't you eat breakfast?

LEE: Look, don't worry about me pal. I can take care a' myself. You just go ahead as though I wasn't even here, all right?

[AUSTIN *goes into kitchen, makes coffee.*]

AUSTIN: Where'd you walk to last night?

[*Pause*]

LEE: I went up in the foothills there. Up in the San Gabriels. Heat was drivin' me crazy.

AUSTIN: Well, wasn't it hot out on the desert?

LEE: Different kinda' heat. Out there it's clean. Cools off at night. There's a nice little breeze.

AUSTIN: Where were you, the Mojave?

LEE: Yeah. The Mojave. That's right.

AUSTIN: I haven't been out there in years.

LEE: Out past Needles there.

AUSTIN: Oh yeah.

LEE: Up here it's different. This country's real different.

AUSTIN: Well, it's been built up.

▷ **1** *classy:* exclusive **2** *Ivy League:* group of leading universities in the USA with social and academic prestige **6** *pal* (AE): friend **11** *the foothills:* low hills • *the San Gabriels:* mountain range in Los Angeles County **15** *breeze:* gentle wind **16** *the Mojave* [mə'hɑːvi]: large desert in south-east California **19** *Needles:* city in south-east California on the border with Arizona

LEE: Built up? Wiped out is more like it. I don't even hardly recognize it.

AUSTIN: Yeah. Foothills are the same though, aren't they?

LEE: Pretty much. It's funny goin' up in there. The smells and everything. Used to catch snakes up there, remember?

AUSTIN: You caught snakes.

LEE: Yeah. And you'd pretend you were Geronimo or some damn thing. You used to go right out to lunch.

AUSTIN: I enjoyed my imagination.

LEE: That what you call it? Looks like yer still enjoyin' it.

AUSTIN: So you just wandered around up there, huh?

LEE: Yeah. With a purpose.

AUSTIN: See any houses?

[*Pause*]

LEE: Couple. Couple a' real nice ones. One of 'em didn't even have a dog. Walked right up and stuck my head in the window. Not a peep. Just a sweet kinda' suburban silence.

AUSTIN: What kind of place was it?

LEE: Like a paradise. Kinda' place that sorta' kills ya' inside. Warm yellow lights. Mexican tile all around. Copper pots hangin' over the stove. Ya' know like they got in the magazines. Blond people movin' in and outa' the rooms, talkin' to each other. [*Pause*] Kinda place you wish you'd sorta' grew up in, ya' know.

AUSTIN: That's the kind of place you wish you'd grown up in?

▷ **1** *wipe sth. out:* destroy sth. completely **4** *pretty much:* nearly, almost **7** *Geronimo* (1829–1909): famous chief of the Apache Indians who fought against white settlers until his capture in 1886 **8** *go right out to lunch* (infml): (here) become totally involved in sth. **12** *purpose:* (here) intention, aim **17** *peep* (n; infml): sound **20** *tile:* Wandfliese

LEE: Yeah, why not?

AUSTIN: I thought you hated that kind of stuff.

LEE: Yeah, well you never knew too much about me did ya'?

[*Pause*]

AUSTIN: Why'd you go out to the desert in the first place?

LEE: I was on my way to see the old man.

AUSTIN: You mean you just passed through there?

LEE: Yeah. That's right. Three months of passin' through.

AUSTIN: Three months?

LEE: Somethin' like that. Maybe more. Why?

AUSTIN: You lived on the Mojave for three months?

LEE: Yeah. What'sa' matter with that?

AUSTIN: By yourself?

LEE: Mostly. Had a couple a' visitors. Had that dog for a while.

AUSTIN: Didn't you miss people?

LEE: [*Laughs*] People?

AUSTIN: Yeah. I mean I go crazy if I have to spend three nights in a motel by myself.

LEE: Yer not in a motel now.

AUSTIN: No, I know. But sometimes I have to stay in motels.

LEE: Well, they got people in motels don't they?

AUSTIN: Strangers.

LEE: Yer friendly aren't ya'? Aren't you the friendly type?

▷ **2** *stuff*: things, objects **5** *in the first place:* at all (used for emphasis)

[*Pause*]

AUSTIN: I'm going to have somebody coming by here later, Lee.

LEE: Ah! Lady friend?

AUSTIN: No, a producer.

LEE: Aha! What's he produce?

AUSTIN: Film. Movies. You know.

LEE: Oh, movies. Motion Pictures! A Big Wig huh?

AUSTIN: Yeah.

LEE: What's he comin' by here for?

AUSTIN: We have to talk about a project.

LEE: Whadya' mean, "a project"? What's "a project"?

AUSTIN: A script.

LEE: Oh. That's what yer doin' with all these papers?

AUSTIN: Yeah.

LEE: Well, what's the project about?

AUSTIN: We're uh – It's a period piece.

LEE: What's "a period piece"?

AUSTIN: Look, it doesn't matter. The main thing is we need to discuss this alone. I mean –

LEE: Oh, I get it. You want me outa' the picture.

AUSTIN: Not exactly. I just need to be alone with him for a couple of hours. So we can talk.

LEE: Yer afraid I'll embarrass ya' huh?

▷ **7** *Big Wig* (infml): person in a leading company who takes important decisions **16** *period piece:* historisches Stück **23** *embarrass sb.:* make sb. ashamed and uncomfortable

AUSTIN: I'm not afraid you'll embarrass me!

LEE: Well, I tell ya' what – Why don't you just gimme the keys to yer car and I'll be back around six o'clock or so. That give ya' enough time?

AUSTIN: I'm not loaning you my car, Lee.

LEE: You want me to just git lost, huh? Take a hike? Is that it? Pound the pavement for a few hours while you bullshit yer way into a million bucks.

AUSTIN: Look, it's going to be hard enough for me to face this character on my own without –

LEE: You don't know this guy?

AUSTIN: No I don't know – He's a producer. I mean I've been meeting with him for months but you never get to know a producer.

LEE: Yer tryin' to hustle him? Is that it?

AUSTIN: I'm not trying to hustle him! I'm trying to work out a deal! It's not easy.

LEE: What kinda' deal?

AUSTIN: Convince him it's a worthwhile story.

LEE: He's not convinced? How come he's comin' over here if he's not convinced? I'll convince him for ya'.

AUSTIN: You don't understand the way things work down here.

LEE: How do things work down here?

[*Pause*]

AUSTIN: Look, if I loan you my car will you have it back here by six?

▷ **5** *loan sb. sth.* (AE): lend sb. sth. **6** *take a hike* (AE infml, derog): go away **6–7** *pound the pavement:* (here) walk around with no aim **7** *bullshit your way into sth.:* talk rubbish in order to get sth. **8** *bucks* (AE): dollars **14** *hustle sb.:* get money from sb. by deceiving them **15** *deal:* agreement

LEE: On the button. With a full tank a' gas.

AUSTIN: [*Digging in his pocket for keys*] Forget about the gas.

LEE: Hey, these days gas is gold, old buddy.

[AUSTIN *hands the keys to* LEE.]

You remember that car I used to loan you?

AUSTIN: Yeah.

LEE: Forty Ford. Flathead.

AUSTIN: Yeah.

LEE: Sucker hauled ass didn't it?

AUSTIN: Lee, it's not that I don't want to loan you my car –

LEE: You are loanin' me yer car.

[LEE *gives* AUSTIN *a pat on the shoulder. Pause.*]

AUSTIN: I know. I just wish –

LEE: What? You wish what?

AUSTIN: I don't know. I wish I wasn't – I wish I didn't have to be doing business down here. I'd like to just spend some time with you.

LEE: I thought it was "Art" you were doin'.

[LEE *moves across the kitchen toward exit, tosses keys in his hand.*]

AUSTIN: Try to get it back here by six, okay?

LEE: No sweat. Hey, ya' know, if that uh – story of yours doesn't go over with the guy – tell him I got a couple a' 'projects' he might be interested in. Real commercial. Full a' suspense. True-to-life stuff.

▷ **1** *on the button* (AE sl): exactly on time **3** *buddy* (AE infml): close friend **7** *Forty Ford:* Ford car from the 1940s • *Flathead:* nickname given to Ford cars due to the shape of their fronts **9** *(the) sucker hauled ass* (sl): the car was very fast **12** *pat:* light touch **18** *toss sth.:* throw sth. lightly in the air **20** *no sweat* [swet] (infml): no problem **20–21** *go over with sb.* (infml): be liked and accepted by sb.

[LEE *exits,* AUSTIN *stares after him then turns, goes to papers at table, leafs through pages, lights fade to black.*]

▷ **2** *leaf through sth.:* etwas durchblättern

Scene Three

Afternoon, alcove, Saul Kimmer *and* Austin *seated across from each other at table.*

Saul: Well, to tell you the truth, Austin, I have never felt so confident about a project in quite a long time.

Austin: Well, that's good to hear, Saul.

Saul: I am absolutely convinced we can get this thing off the ground. I mean we'll have to make a sale to television and that means getting a major star. Somebody bankable. But I think we can do it. I really do.

Austin: Don't you think we need a first draft before we approach a star?

Saul: No, no, not at all. I don't think it's necessary. Maybe a brief synopsis. I don't want you to touch the typewriter until we have some seed money.

Austin: That's fine with me.

Saul: I mean it's a great story. Just the story alone. You've really managed to capture something this time.

Austin: I'm glad you like it, Saul.

[Lee *enters abruptly into kitchen carrying a stolen television set. Short pause.*]

Lee: Aw shit, I'm sorry about that. I am really sorry, Austin.

▷ **3** *confident:* optimistic **6** *get sth. off the ground* (infml): start sth. that will be successful **8** *someboby bankable:* (here) actor who is famous enough to make people want to see a movie so that it makes money **10** *draft:* rough sketch or outline **13** *synopsis* [sɪ'nɑːpsɪs]: summary **14** *seed money* (AE): Grundkapital **17** *capture sth.:* (here) succeed in expressing a feeling, an atmosphere, etc., esp. in a novel or movie **19** *abruptly:* suddenly and unexpectedly

AUSTIN: [*Standing*] That's all right.

LEE: [*Moving toward them*] I mean I thought it was way past six already. You said to have it back here by six.

AUSTIN: We were just finishing up. [*To* SAUL] This is my uh – brother, Lee.

SAUL: [*Standing*] Oh, I'm very happy to meet you.

[LEE *sets TV on sink counter, shakes hands with* SAUL.]

LEE: I can't tell ya' how happy I am to meet you, sir.

SAUL: Saul Kimmer.

LEE: Mr Kipper.

SAUL: Kimmer.

AUSTIN: Lee's been living out on the desert and he just uh –

SAUL: Oh, that's terrific! [*To* LEE] Palm Springs?

LEE: Yeah. Yeah, right. Right around in that area. Near uh – Bob Hope Drive there.

SAUL: Oh I love it out there. I just love it. The air is wonderful.

LEE: Yeah. Sure is. Healthy.

SAUL: And the golf. I don't know if you play golf, but the golf is just about the best.

LEE: I play a lota' golf.

SAUL: Is that right?

LEE: Yeah. In fact I was hoping I'd run into somebody out here who played a little golf. I've been lookin' for a partner.

▷ **2** *way past six:* a long time after six o'clock **10** *kipper:* Räucherhering **13** *Palm Springs:* resort city in southern California very popular with Hollywood movie stars and millionaires **14** *Bob Hope* (1903–2003): famous US actor and comedian **15** *drive:* road **22** *run into sb.:* happen to meet sb.

SAUL: Well, I uh –

AUSTIN: Lee's just down for a visit while our mother's in Alaska.

SAUL: Oh, your mother's in Alaska?

AUSTIN: Yes. She went up there on a little vacation. This is her place.

SAUL: I see. Well isn't that something. Alaska.

LEE: What kinda' handicap do ya' have, Mr Kimmer?

SAUL: Oh I'm just a Sunday duffer really. You know.

LEE: That's good 'cause I haven't swung a club in months.

SAUL: Well we ought to get together sometime and have a little game. Austin, do you play? [SAUL *mimes a Johnny Carson golf swing for* AUSTIN.]

AUSTIN: No. I don't uh – I've watched it on TV.

LEE: [*To* SAUL] How 'bout tomorrow morning? Bright and early. We could get out there and put in eighteen holes before breakfast.

SAUL: Well, I've got uh – I have several appointments –

LEE: No, I mean real early. Crack a' dawn. While the dew's still thick on the fairway.

SAUL: Sounds really great.

LEE: Austin could be our caddie.

SAUL: Now that's an idea. [*Laughs*]

▷ **5** *isn't that something:* isn't that interesting/great? **7** *Sunday duffer* (sl): person who is not very good at sth., as they only play for fun (e.g. on Sundays) **8** *club:* stick used for hitting a golf ball **10** *Johnny Carson* (1925–2005): well-known TV entertainer, who swung an imaginary golf club at the end of his opening monologues on his TV show **14** *put in eighteen holes:* play through the entire golf course **15** *appointment:* meeting **16** *(at the) crack of dawn* (infml): very early in the morning • *dew:* Tau **17** *fairway:* particular area on a golf-course **19** *caddie:* person who carries the clubs of a golfer during a game

AUSTIN: I don't know the first thing about golf.

LEE: There's nothin' to it. Isn't that right, Saul? He'd pick it up in fifteen minutes.

SAUL: Sure. Doesn't take long. 'Course you have to play for years to find your true form. [*Chuckles*]

LEE: [*To* AUSTIN] We'll give ya' a quick run-down on the club faces. The irons, the woods. Show ya' a couple pointers on the basic swing. Might even let ya' hit the ball a couple times. Whadya' think, Saul?

SAUL: Why not. I think it'd be great. I haven't had any exercise in weeks.

LEE: 'At's the spirit! We'll have a little orange juice right afterwards.

[*Pause*]

SAUL: Orange juice?

LEE: Yeah! Vitamin C! Nothin' like a shot a'orange juice after a round a' golf. Hot shower. Snappin' towels at each other's privates. Real sense a' fraternity.

SAUL: [*Smiles at* AUSTIN] Well, you make it sound very inviting, I must say. It really does sound great.

LEE: Then it's a date.

SAUL: Well, I'll call the country club and see if I can arrange something.

LEE: Great! Boy, I sure am sorry that I busted in on ya' all in the middle of yer meeting.

▷ **2** *pick sth. up:* learn sth. quickly by doing it **5** *chuckle:* laugh quietly **6** *run-down:* outline • *club face:* Schlagfläche des Golfschlägers **7** *iron, wood:* the names of two types of clubs • *pointer:* tip, hint, advice **12** *that's the spirit:* that's the right attitude **15** *shot:* small drink **16** *snap sth.:* etwas als Peitsche benutzen • *privates* (infml): genitals **17** *sense of fraternity* (fml): feeling of brotherhood among a group of people **20** *it's a date:* it's agreed **23** *bust in on sb.* (AE sl): disturb or interrupt sb.

SAUL: Oh that's quite all right. We were just about finished anyway.

LEE: I can wait out in the other room if you want.

SAUL: No really –

LEE: Just got Austin's color TV back from the shop. I can watch a little amateur boxing now.

[LEE *and* AUSTIN *exchange looks.*]

SAUL: Oh – Yes.

LEE: You don't fool around in Television, do you Saul?

SAUL: Uh – I have in the past. Produced some TV Specials. Network stuff. But it's mainly features now.

LEE: That's where the big money is, huh?

SAUL: Yes. That's right.

AUSTIN: Why don't I call you tomorrow, Saul, and we'll get together. We can have lunch or something.

SAUL: That'd be terrific.

LEE: Right after the golf.

[*Pause*]

SAUL: What?

LEE: You can have lunch right after the golf.

SAUL: Oh, right.

LEE: Austin was tellin' me that yer interested in stories.

SAUL: Well, we develop certain projects that we feel have commercial potential.

LEE: What kinda' stuff do ya' go in for?

▷ **24** *go in for sth.:* have an interest in sth.; work with sth.

SAUL: Oh, the usual. You know. Good love interest. Lots of action. [*Chuckles at* AUSTIN]

LEE: Westerns?

SAUL: Sometimes.

AUSTIN: I'll give you a ring, Saul.

[AUSTIN *tries to move* SAUL *across the kitchen but* LEE *blocks their way.*]

LEE: I got a Western that'd knock yer lights out.

SAUL: Oh really?

LEE: Yeah. Contemporary Western. Based on a true story. 'Course I'm not a writer like my brother here. I'm not a man of the pen.

SAUL: Well –

LEE: I mean I can tell ya' a story off the tongue but I can't put it down on paper. That don't make any difference though, does it?

SAUL: No, not really.

LEE: I mean plenty a' guys have stories don't they? True-life stories. Musta' been a lota' movies made from real life.

SAUL: Yes. I suppose so.

LEE: I haven't seen a good western since *Lonely Are the Brave*. You remember that movie?

SAUL: No, I'm afraid I –

LEE: Kirk Douglas. Helluva' movie. You remember that movie, Austin?

AUSTIN: Yes.

▷ **5** *ring* (n): telephone call **8** *that'd knock your lights out* (sl): der Sie vom Hocker hauen würde **13** *off the tongue* (infml): verbally **19** *Lonely Are the Brave:* famous western movie (1962) **22** *Kirk Douglas* (born 1916): US movie star

LEE: [*To* SAUL] The man dies for the love of a horse.

SAUL: Is that right.

LEE: Yeah. Ya' hear the horse screamin' at the end of it. Rain comin' down. Horse screamin'. Then there's a shot. BLAM! Just a single shot like that. Then nothin' but the sound of rain. And Kirk Douglas is ridin' in the ambulance. Ridin' away from the scene of the accident. And when he hears that shot he knows that his horse has died. He knows. And you see his eyes. And his eyes die. Right inside his face. And then his eyes close. And you know that he's died too. You know that Kirk Douglas has died from the death of his horse.

SAUL: [*Eyes* AUSTIN *nervously*] Well, it sounds like a great movie. I'm sorry I missed it.

LEE: Yeah, you shouldn't a' missed that one.

SAUL: I'll have to try to catch it some time. Arrange a screening or something. Well, Austin, I'll have to hit the freeway before rush hour.

AUSTIN: [*Ushers* SAUL *toward exit*] It's good seeing you, Saul.

[AUSTIN *and* SAUL *shake hands.*]

LEE: So ya' think there's room for a real Western these days? A true-to-life Western?

SAUL: Well, I don't see why not. Why don't you uh – tell the story to Austin and have him write a little outline.

LEE: You'd take a look at it then?

SAUL: Yes. Sure. I'll give it a read-through. Always eager for new material. [*Smiles at* AUSTIN]

▷ **15** *catch sth.* (AE sl): see sth. (esp. a film or play) • *arrange a screening:* organize a (private) showing of a movie **16** *hit the freeway* (AE infml): be on the motorway; (here) leave **18** *usher sb.:* lead sb. to the place where he should go **25** *give sth. a read-through:* read through sth. quickly to form an impression of it

LEE: That's great! You'd really read it then, huh?

SAUL: It would just be my opinion of course.

LEE: That's all I want. Just an opinion. I happen to think it has a lota' possibilities.

SAUL: Well, it was great meeting you and I'll –

[SAUL *and* LEE *shake.*]

LEE: I'll call you tomorrow about the golf.

SAUL: Oh. Yes, right.

LEE: Austin's got your number, right?

SAUL: Yes.

LEE: So long, Saul.

[LEE *gives* SAUL *a pat on the back.* SAUL *exits,* AUSTIN *turns to* LEE, *looks at TV, then back to* LEE.]

AUSTIN: Give me the keys.

[AUSTIN *extends his hand toward* LEE, LEE *doesn't move, just stares at* AUSTIN, *smiles. Lights to black.*]

▷ **11** *so long* (AE infml): goodbye

SCENE FOUR

Night, coyotes in distance, fade, sound of typewriter in dark, crickets, candle-light in alcove, dim light in kitchen. Lights reveal AUSTIN *at glass table typing,* LEE *sits across from him, foot on table, drinking beer and whiskey; the TV is still on sink counter,* AUSTIN *types for a while then stops.*

LEE: All right, now read it back to me.

AUSTIN: I'm not reading it back to you, Lee. You can read it when we're finished. I can't spend all night on this.

LEE: You got better things to do?

AUSTIN: Let's just go ahead. Now what happens when he leaves Texas?

LEE: Is he ready to leave Texas yet? I didn't know we were that far along. He's not ready to leave Texas.

AUSTIN: He's right at the border.

LEE: [*Sitting up*] No, see, this is one a' the crucial parts. Right here. [*Taps paper with beer can.*] We can't rush through this. He's not right at the border. He's a good fifty miles from the border. A lot can happen in fifty miles.

AUSTIN: It's only an outline. We're not writing an entire script now.

LEE: Well ya' can't leave things out even if it is an outline. It's one a' the most important parts. Ya' can't go leavin' it out.

AUSTIN: Okay, okay. Let's just – get it done.

LEE: All right. Now. He's in the truck and he's got his horse trailer and his horse.

▷ **1** *fade:* become quieter **2** *dim:* not bright **10** *go ahead:* continue **15** *crucial:* of great importance **19** *entire* [ɪn'taɪər]: whole, complete **23** *truck* (AE): lorry • *horse trailer:* vehicle to transport horses

Austin: We've already established that.

Lee: And he sees this other guy comin' up behind him in another truck. And that truck is pullin' a gooseneck.

Austin: What's a gooseneck?

Lee: Cattle trailer. You know the kind with a gooseneck, goes right down in the bed a' the pick-up.

Austin: Oh. All right. [*Types*]

Lee: It's important.

Austin: Okay. I got it.

Lee: All these details are important.

[Austin *types as they talk.*]

Austin: I've got it.

Lee: And this other guy's got his horse all saddled up in the back a' the gooseneck.

Austin: Right.

Lee: So both these guys have got their horses right along with 'em, see.

Austin: I understand.

Lee: Then this first guy suddenly realizes two things.

Austin: The guy in front?

Lee: Right. The guy in front realizes two things almost at the same time: Simultaneous.

Austin: What were the two things?

▷ **3** *gooseneck:* trailer that is lower to the ground than the truck and thus needs a coupling (= Kupplung) shaped like the neck of a goose **5–6** *go right down in the bed* (AE infml): fit exactly **6** *pick-up* (n): small van with low sides and no roof at the back

LEE: Number one, he realizes that the guy behind him is the husband of the woman he's been – [LEE *makes gesture of screwing by pumping his arm.*]

AUSTIN: [*Sees* LEE's *gesture*] Oh. Yeah.

LEE: And number two, he realizes he's in the middle of Tornado Country.

AUSTIN: What's 'Tornado Country'?

LEE: Panhandle.

AUSTIN: Panhandle?

LEE: Sweetwater. Around in that area. Nothin'. Nowhere. And number three –

AUSTIN: I thought there was only two.

LEE: There's three. There's a third unforeseen realization.

AUSTIN: And what's that?

LEE: That he's runnin' outa' gas.

AUSTIN: [*Stops typing*] Come on, Lee. [*He gets up, moves to kitchen, gets a glass of water.*]

LEE: Whadya' mean, 'come on'? That's what it is. Write it down! He's runnin' outa' gas.

AUSTIN: It's too –

LEE: What? It's too what? It's too real! That's what ya' mean isn't it? It's too much like real life!

AUSTIN: It's not like real life! It's not enough like real life. Things don't happen like that.

▷ **2** *screw sb.* (sl): have sexual intercourse with sb. **3** *pump sth.* (infml): (here) move sth. powerfully up and down **8** *Panhandle:* area of northern Texas, which is long and narrow (like the handle of a pan) **10** *Sweetwater:* town in west-central Texas **15** *run out of sth.:* finish your supply of sth. • *gas* (AE): petrol

LEE: What! Men don't fuck other men's women?

AUSTIN: Yes. But they don't end up chasing each other across the Panhandle. Through 'Tornado Country'.

LEE: They do in this movie!

AUSTIN: And they don't have horses conveniently along with them when they run out of gas! And they don't run out of gas either!

LEE: These guys run outa' gas! This is my story and one a' these guys runs outa' gas!

AUSTIN: It's just a dumb excuse to get them into a chase scene. It's contrived.

LEE: It is a chase scene! It's already a chase scene. They been chasin' each other fer days.

AUSTIN: So now they're supposed to abandon their trucks, climb on their horses and chase each other into the mountains?

LEE: [*Standing suddenly*] There aren't any mountains in the Panhandle! It's flat!! [*He turns violently toward windows in alcove and throws beer can at them.*] Goddamn these crickets! [*Yells at crickets*] Shut up out there! [*Pause, turns back toward table.*] This place is like a fuckin' rest home here. How're you supposed to think!

AUSTIN: You wanna' take a break!

LEE: No, I don't wanna' take a break! I wanna' get this done! This is my last chance to get this done.

AUSTIN: [*Moves back into alcove*] All right. Take it easy.

LEE: I'm gonna' be leavin' this area. I don't have time to mess around here.

▷ **5** *conveniently* (here): fortunately and purely by chance **10** *contrived:* artificial **13** *abandon sth.:* leave sth. behind **19** *rest home:* home for old people **25** *mess around:* waste your time

AUSTIN: Where are you going?

LEE: Never mind where I'm goin'! That's got nothin' to do with you. I just gotta' get this done. I'm not like you. Hangin' around bein' a parasite offa' other fools. I gotta' do this thing and get out.

[*Pause*]

AUSTIN: A parasite? Me?

LEE: Yeah, you!

AUSTIN: After you break into people's houses and take their televisions?

LEE: They don't need their televisions! I'm doin' them a service.

AUSTIN: Give me back my keys, Lee.

LEE: Not until you write this thing! You're gonna' write this outline thing for me or that car's gonna wind up in Arizona with a different paint job.

AUSTIN: You think you can force me to write this? I was doing you a favor.

LEE: Git off yer high horse will ya'! Favor! Big favor. Handin' down favors from the mountain top.

AUSTIN: Let's just write it, okay? Let's sit down and not get upset and see if we can just get through this.

[AUSTIN *sits at typewriter. Long pause.*]

LEE: Yer not gonna' even show it to him, are ya'?

AUSTIN: What?

LEE: This outline. You got no intention of showin' it to him. Yer just doin' this 'cause yer afraid a' me.

▷ **4** *offa'* (non-standard): off **13** *wind up* [waɪnd] (infml): end up **13–14** *a different paint job* (infml): a different colour **17** *get off your high horse:* von seinem hohen Ross herunterkommen

AUSTIN: You can show it to him yourself.

LEE: I will, boy! I'm gonna' read it to him on the golf course.

AUSTIN: And I'm not afraid of you either.

LEE: Then how come yer doin' it?

AUSTIN: [*Pause.*] So I can get my keys back.

[*Pause as* LEE *takes keys out of his pocket slowly and throws them on table. Long pause.* AUSTIN *stares at keys.*]

LEE: There. Now you got yer keys back.

[AUSTIN *looks up at* LEE *but doesn't take keys.*]

Go ahead. There's yer keys.

[AUSTIN *slowly takes keys off table and puts them back in his own pocket.*]

Now what're you gonna' do? Kick me out?

AUSTIN: I'm not going to kick you out, Lee.

LEE: You couldn't kick me out, boy.

AUSTIN: I know.

LEE: So you can't even consider that one. [*Pause.*] You could call the Police. That'd be the obvious thing.

AUSTIN: You're my brother.

LEE: That don't mean a thing. You go down to the L.A. Police Department there and ask them what kinda' people kill each other most. What do you think they'd say?

AUSTIN: Who said anything about killing?

▷ **4** *how come* (infml): used to ask the reason for sth. **17** *that one:* (here) that idea **18** *obvious:* plausible, easy to understand **20** *L.A.:* Los Angeles

LEE: Family people. Brothers. Brothers-in-Law. Cousins. Real American-type people. They kill each other in the heat mostly. In the Smog-Alerts. In the Brush-Fire Season. Right about this time a' year.

AUSTIN: This isn't the same.

LEE: Oh no? What makes it different?

AUSTIN: We're not insane. We're not driven to acts of violence like that. Not over a dumb movie script. Now sit down.

[*Long pause,* LEE *considers which way to go with it.*]

LEE: Maybe not. [*He sits back down at table across from* AUSTIN.] Maybe you're right. Maybe we're too intelligent, huh? [*Pause.*] We got our heads on our shoulders. One of us has even got a Ivy League diploma. Now that means somethin' don't it? Doesn't that mean somethin'?

AUSTIN: Look, I'll write this thing for you, Lee. I don't mind writing it. I just don't want to get all worked up about it. It's not worth it. Now, come on. Let's just get through it, okay?

LEE: Nah. I think there's easier money. Lotsa' places I could pick up thousands. Maybe millions. I don't need this shit. I could go up to Sacramento Valley and steal me a diesel. Ten thousand a week dismantling one a' those suckers. Ten thousand a week! [*He opens another beer, puts his foot back up on table.*]

AUSTIN: No, really, look, I'll write it out for you. I think it's a great idea.

LEE: Nah, you got yer own work to do. I don't wanna' interfere with yer life.

▷ **3** *alert* [ə'lɜːrt]: alarm • *brush:* Unterholz, Gestrüpp **7** *insane:* mentally ill **12** *have your head on your shoulders:* be sensible and reasonable **15** *not mind doing sth.:* be willing to do sth. **16** *get all worked up:* get very excited and angry **21** *dismantle sth.:* take sth. apart • *sucker* (derog sl): thing; (here) car **24** *interfere with sth.:* get in the way of sth.

AUSTIN: I mean it'd be really fantastic if you could sell this. Turn it into a movie. I mean it.

[*Pause*]

LEE: Ya' think so, huh?

AUSTIN: Absolutely. You could really turn your life around, you know. Change things.

LEE: I could get me a house maybe.

AUSTIN: Sure you could get a house. You could get a whole ranch if you wanted to.

LEE: [*Laughs*] A ranch? I could get a ranch?

AUSTIN: 'Course you could. You know what a screenplay sells for these days?

LEE: No. What's it sell for?

AUSTIN: A lot. A whole lot of money.

LEE: Thousands?

AUSTIN: Yeah. Thousands.

LEE: Millions?

AUSTIN: Well –

LEE: We could get the old man outa' hock then.

AUSTIN: Maybe.

LEE: Maybe? Whadya' mean, maybe?

AUSTIN: I mean it might take more than money.

LEE: You were just tellin' me it'd change my whole life around. Why wouldn't it change his?

▷ **11** *screenplay:* movie script **19** *get sb. out of hock* (infml): help sb. get rid of their debts

AUSTIN: He's different.

LEE: Oh, he's of a different ilk, huh?

AUSTIN: He's not gonna' change. Let's leave the old man out of it.

LEE: That's right. He's not gonna' change but I will. I'll just turn myself right inside out. I could be just like you then, huh? Sittin' around dreamin' stuff up. Gettin' paid to dream. Ridin' back and forth on the freeway just dreamin' my fool head off.

AUSTIN: It's not all that easy.

LEE: It's not, huh?

AUSTIN: No. There's a lot of work involved.

LEE: What's the toughest part? Deciding whether to jog or play tennis?

[*Long pause.*]

AUSTIN: Well, look. You can stay here – do whatever you want to. Borrow the car. Come in and out. Doesn't matter to me. It's not my house. I'll help you write this thing or – not. Just let me know what you want. You tell me.

LEE: Oh. So now suddenly you're at my service. Is that it?

AUSTIN: What do you want to do, Lee?

[*Long pause.* LEE *stares at him then turns and dreams at windows.*]

LEE: I tell ya' what I'd do if I still had that dog. Ya' wanna' know what I'd do?

AUSTIN: What?

LEE: Head out to Ventura. Cook up a little match. God that little dog could bear down. Lota' money in dog fightin'. Big money.

▷ **2** *be of a different ilk* (infml): be a different type **7** *fool:* foolish **11** *tough* [tʌf]: difficult **23** *head out to sth.* (infml): move towards sth. • *Ventura:* city in south-western California on the Pacific Coast • *cook sth. up* (AE infml): plan and prepare sth. **24** *bear down:* (here) attack

[*Pause*]

AUSTIN: Why don't we try to see this through, Lee. Just for the hell of it. Maybe you've really got something here. What do you think?

[*Pause.* LEE *considers.*]

LEE: Maybe so. No harm in tryin' I guess. You think it's such a hot idea. Besides, I always wondered what'd be like to be you.

AUSTIN: You did?

LEE: Yeah, sure. I used to picture you walkin' around some campus with yer arms fulla' books. Blondes chasin' after ya'.

AUSTIN: Blondes? That's funny.

LEE: What's funny about it?

AUSTIN: Because I always used to picture you somewhere.

LEE: Where'd you picture me?

AUSTIN: Oh, I don't know. Different places. Adventures. You were always on some adventure.

LEE: Yeah.

AUSTIN: And I used to say to myself, "Lee's got the right idea. He's out there in the world and here I am. What am I doing?"

LEE: Well you were settin' yourself up for somethin'.

AUSTIN: I guess.

LEE: We better get started on this thing then.

AUSTIN: Okay. [*He sits up at typewriter, puts new paper in.*]

▷ **2–3** *for the hell of it* (infml): for fun **20** *set yourself up for sth.:* establish yourself in sth. (important)

LEE: Oh. Can I get the keys back before I forget?

[AUSTIN *hesitates.*]

You said I could borrow the car if I wanted, right? Isn't that what you said?

AUSTIN: Yeah. Right.

[AUSTIN *takes keys out of his pocket, sets them on table,* LEE *takes keys slowly, plays with them in his hand.*]

LEE: I could get a ranch, huh?

AUSTIN: Yeah. We have to write it first though.

LEE: Okay. Let's write it.

[*Lights start dimming slowly to end of scene as* AUSTIN *types,* LEE *speaks.*]

So they take off after each other straight into an endless black prairie. The sun is just comin' down and they can feel the night on their backs. What they don't know is that each one of 'em is afraid see. Each one separately thinks that he's the only one that's afraid. And they keep ridin' like that straight into the night. Not knowing. And the one who's chasin' doesn't know where the other one is taking him. And the one who's being chased doesn't know where he's going.

[*Lights to black, typing stops in the dark, crickets fade. Music in Act break: Hank Williams' "Ramblin' Man".*]

▷ **11** *dim* (v): become gradually darker **13** *take off after sb./sth.:* start to chase sb./sth. **16** *see:* you understand? **22** *Hank Williams* (1923–1953): US country-and-western singer • *rambling man:* man who cannot settle down

ACT TWO

SCENE FIVE

Morning, LEE *at table in alcove with a set of golf clubs in a fancy leather bag,* AUSTIN *at sink washing a few dishes.*

AUSTIN: He really liked it, huh?

LEE: He wouldn't a' gave me these clubs if he didn't like it.

AUSTIN: He gave you the clubs?

LEE: Yeah. I told ya' he gave me the clubs. The bag too.

AUSTIN: I thought he just loaned them to you.

LEE: He said it was part a' the advance. A little gift like. Gesture of his good faith.

AUSTIN: He's giving you an advance?

LEE: Now what's so amazing about that? I told ya' it was a good story. You even said it was a good story.

AUSTIN: Well that is really incredible, Lee. You know how many guys spend their whole lives down here trying to break into this business? Just trying to get in the door?

LEE: [*Pulling clubs out of bag, testing them*] I got no idea. How many?

[*Pause*]

AUSTIN: How much of an advance is he giving you?

▷ **1** *fancy* (adj): expensive-looking **8** *advance* (n): Vorauszahlung • *a little gift like:* (it was) like a / a sort of little present **8–9** *gesture of good faith:* sign of good will showing that you can trust sb./sth. **13** *incredible:* extremely good, but hard to believe

LEE: Plenty. We were talkin' big money out there. Ninth hole is where I sealed the deal.

AUSTIN: He made a firm commitment?

LEE: Absolutely.

AUSTIN: Well, I know Saul and he doesn't fool around when he says he likes something.

LEE: I thought you said you didn't know him.

AUSTIN: Well, I'm familiar with his tastes.

LEE: I let him get two up on me goin' into the back nine. He was sure he had me cold. You shoulda' seen his face when I pulled out the old pitching wedge and plopped it pin-high, two feet from the cup. He 'bout shit his pants. "Where'd a guy like you ever learn how to play golf like that?" he says.

[LEE *laughs*, AUSTIN *stares at him.*]

AUSTIN: 'Course there's no contract yet. Nothing's final until it's on paper.

LEE: It's final, all right. There's no way he's gonna' back out of it now. We gambled for it.

AUSTIN: Saul, gambled?

LEE: Yeah, sure. I mean he liked the outline already so he wasn't risking that much. I just guaranteed it with my short game.

[*Pause*]

▷ **2** *seal a deal:* settle a business transaction **3** *firm commitment:* definite promise to do sth. **9** *get two up on sb.:* be ahead by two points in a game • *back nine:* the last nine holes on a golf-course **10** *have sb. cold* (infml): beat sb. easily **11** *pitching wedge:* iron golf club used for hitting the ball high or out of a bunker • *plop the ball pin-high, two feet from the cup*: hit the ball so that it lands two feet from the hole **12** *he 'bout shit his pants = he almost shit his pants* (sl): he was totally surprised **17** *back out of sth.:* withdraw from sth. (e.g. a deal, an agreement) **19** *gamble:* wetten

AUSTIN: Well, we should celebrate or something. I think Mom left a bottle of Champagne in the refrigerator. We should have a little toast.

[AUSTIN *gets glasses from cupboard, goes to refrigerator, pulls out bottle of Champagne.*]

LEE: You shouldn't oughta' take her Champagne, Austin. She's gonna' miss that.

AUSTIN: Oh, she's not going to mind. She'd be glad we put it to good use. I'll get her another bottle. Besides, it's perfect for the occasion.

[*Pause*]

LEE: Yer gonna' get a nice fee fer writin' the script a' course. Straight fee.

[AUSTIN *stops, stares at* LEE, *puts glasses and bottle on table. Pause.*]

AUSTIN: I'm writing the script?

LEE: That's what he said. Said we couldn't hire a better screenwriter in the whole town.

AUSTIN: But I'm already working on a script. I've got my own project. I don't have time to write two scripts.

LEE: No, he said he was gonna' drop that other one.

[*Pause*]

AUSTIN: What? You mean mine? He's going to drop mine and do yours instead?

LEE: [*Smiles*] Now look, Austin, it's jest beginner's luck ya' know. I mean I sank a fifty-foot putt for this deal. No hard feelings.

▷ **2–3** *have a toast:* (auf etwas) anstoßen **6** *shouldn't oughta'* (non-standard): shouldn't have **8** *not mind:* not care, not worry **11** *fee:* (here) payment • *straight:* (here) good **19** *drop sth.* (infml): give sth. up **24** *sink a fifty-foot putt* [pʌt]: get the ball into the hole without hitting it in the air • *no hard feelings:* used to tell sb. who you have beaten in a game or contest that you would still like to be friends with them

[AUSTIN *goes to phone on wall, grabs it, starts dialing.*]

He's not gonna' be in, Austin. Told me he wouldn't be in 'til late this afternoon.

AUSTIN: [*Stays on phone, dialing, listens*] I can't believe this. I just can't believe it. Are you sure he said that? Why would he drop mine?

LEE: That's what he told me.

AUSTIN: He can't do that without telling me first. Without talking to me at least. He wouldn't just make a decision like that without talking to me!

LEE: Well I was kinda' surprised myself. But he was real enthusiastic about my story.

[AUSTIN *hangs up phone violently, paces.*]

AUSTIN: What'd he say! Tell me everything he said!

LEE: I been tellin' ya'! He said he liked the story a whole lot. It was the first authentic Western to come along in a decade.

AUSTIN: He liked that story? Your story?

LEE: Yeah! What's so surprisin' about that?

AUSTIN: It's stupid! It's the dumbest story I ever heard in my life.

LEE: Hey, hold on! That's my story yer talkin' about!

AUSTIN: It's a bullshit story! It's idiotic. Two lamebrains chasing each other across Texas! Are you kidding? Who do you think's going to go see a film like that?

LEE: It's not a film! It's a movie. There's a big difference. That's somethin' Saul told me.

AUSTIN: Oh he did, huh?

▷ **13** *pace:* walk to and fro with regular steps **21** *lamebrain* (AE infml): stupid person **22** *kid* (v; infml, here: derog): make a joke

LEE: Yeah, he said, "In this business we make Movies, American Movies. Leave the Films to the French."

AUSTIN: So you got real intimate with old Saul, huh? He started pouring forth his vast knowledge of Cinema.

LEE: I think he liked me a lot, to tell ya' the truth. I think he felt I was somebody he could confide in.

AUSTIN: What'd you do, beat him up or something?

LEE: [*Stands fast*] Hey, I've about had it with the insults, buddy! You think yer the only one in the brain department here? Yer the only one that can sit around and cook things up? There's other people got ideas too, ya' know!

AUSTIN: You must've done something. Threatened him or something. Now what'd you do, Lee?

LEE: I convinced him!

[LEE *makes sudden menacing lunge toward* AUSTIN, *wielding golf club above his head, stops himself, frozen moment, long pause.* LEE *lowers club.*]

AUSTIN: Oh, Jesus. You didn't hurt him, did you?

[*Long silence,* LEE *sits back down at table.*]

Lee! Did you hurt him?

LEE: I didn't do nothin' to him! He liked my story. Pure and simple. He said it was the best story he's come across in a long, long time.

AUSTIN: That's what he told me about my story! That's the same thing he said to me.

▷ **4** *pour forth* (fml): express in a pedantic way **6** *confide in sb.:* trust sb.; be able to tell sb. important (and personal) things **7** *beat sb. up:* hit sb. hard and often **8** *I've about had it with sth.* (infml): I've had enough of sth. (*about = just about:* nearly) **10** *cook things up* (infml): invent a story, etc. (quickly) **15** *wield sth.* [wiːld]: hold sth., as if to use it as a weapon

LEE: Well, he musta' been lyin'. He musta' been lyin' to one of us anyway.

AUSTIN: You can't come into this town and start pushing people around. They're gonna' put you away!

LEE: I never pushed anybody around! I beat him fair and square. [*Pause*] They can't touch me anyway. They can't put a finger on me. I'm gone. I can come in through the window and go out through the door. They never knew what hit 'em. You, yer stuck. Yer the one that's stuck. Not me. So don't be warnin' me what to do in this town.

[*Pause,* AUSTIN *crosses to table, sits at typewriter, rests.*]

AUSTIN: Lee come on, level with me will you? It doesn't make any sense that suddenly he'd throw my idea out the window. I've been talking to him for months. I've got too much at stake. Everything's riding on this project.

LEE: What's yer idea?

AUSTIN: It's just a simple love story.

LEE: What kinda' love story?

AUSTIN: [*Stands, crosses into kitchen*] I'm not telling you!

LEE: Ha! 'Fraid I'll steal it, huh? Competition's gettin' kinda' close to home isn't it?

AUSTIN: Where did Saul say he was going?

LEE: He was gonna' take my story to a couple studios.

AUSTIN: That's *my* outline you know! I wrote that outline! You've got no right to be peddling it around.

▷ **4** *put sb. away* (infml): put sb. in prison **5** *fair and square:* honestly and according to the rules **8** *be stuck:* be unable to move **12** *level with sb.* (infml): not hide facts from sb., be honest with sb. **14** *at stake:* at risk **15** *ride on sth.* (infml): depend on sth. **25** *peddle sth. around:* mit etwas hausieren gehen

LEE: You weren't ready to take credit for it last night.

AUSTIN: Give me my keys!

LEE: What?

AUSTIN: The keys! I want my keys back!

LEE: Where you goin'?

AUSTIN: Just give me my keys! I gotta' take a drive. I gotta' get out of here for a while.

LEE: Where you gonna' go, Austin?

AUSTIN: [*Pause*] I might just drive out to the desert for a while. I gotta' think.

LEE: You can think here just as good. This is the perfect set-up for thinkin'. We got some writin' to do here, boy. Now let's just have us a little toast. Relax. We're partners now.

[LEE *pops the cork of the Champagne bottle, pours two drinks as the lights fade to black.*]

▷ **1** *take credit for sth.:* accept praise or approval for sth. for which you are responsible **11** *set-up* (n; infml): place

Scene Six

Afternoon, Lee *and* Saul *in kitchen,* Austin *in alcove.*

Lee: Now you tell him. You tell him, Mr Kipper.

Saul: Kimmer.

Lee: Kimmer. You tell him what you told me. He don't believe me.

Austin: I don't want to hear it.

Saul: It's really not a big issue. Austin. I was simply amazed by your brother's story and –

Austin: Amazed? You lost a bet! You gambled with my material!

Saul: That's really beside the point, Austin. I'm ready to go all the way with your brother's story. I think it has a great deal of merit.

Austin: I don't want to hear about it, okay? Go tell it to the executives! Tell it to somebody who's going to turn it into a package deal or something. A TV series. Don't tell it to me.

Saul: But I want to continue with your project too, Austin. It's not as though we can't do both. We're big enough for that aren't we?

Austin: "We"? *I* can't do both! I don't know about "we".

Lee: [*To* Saul] See, what'd I tell ya'. He's totally unsympathetic.

Saul: Austin, there's no point in our going to another screenwriter for this. It just doesn't make sense. You're brothers. You know each other. There's a familiarity with material that just wouldn't be possible otherwise.

▷ **6** *issue* [ˈɪʃuː]: matter, affair **9** *that's beside the point:* that's irrelevant **10** *merit:* (here) good quality that deserves respect **11–12** *executive* (n): person running a company **12** *package deal:* Paket **17** *unsympathetic:* not supportive of an idea **18** *there's no point in doing sth.:* it's no use doing sth.

AUSTIN: There's no familiarity with the material! None! I don't know what "Tornado Country" is. I don't know what a "gooseneck" is. And I don't want to know! [*Pointing to* LEE] He's a hustler! He's a bigger hustler than you are! If you can't see that, then –

LEE: [*To* AUSTIN] Hey, now hold on. I didn't have to bring this bone back to you, boy. I persuaded Saul here that you were the right man for the job. You don't have to go throwin' up favors in my face.

AUSTIN: Favors! I'm the one who wrote the fuckin' outline! You can't even spell.

SAUL: [*To* AUSTIN] Your brother told me about the situation with your father.

[*Pause*]

AUSTIN: What? [*Looks at* LEE.]

SAUL: That's right. Now we have a clear cut deal here, Austin. We have big studio money standing behind this thing. Just on the basis of your outline.

AUSTIN: [*To* SAUL] What'd he tell you about my father?

SAUL: Well – that he's destitute. He needs money.

LEE: That's right. He does.

[AUSTIN *shakes his head, stares at them both.*]

AUSTIN: [*To* LEE] And this little assignment is supposed to go toward the old man? A charity project? Is that what this is? Did you cook this up on the ninth green too?

SAUL: It's a big slice, Austin.

▷ **4** *hustler* (AE infml): person who sells or gets sth. by acting dishonestly or by putting pressure on people **5** *hold on* (infml): wait a minute; just a moment • *bone* (sl): (here) golden opportunity, lucky chance **18** *destitute:* poor, without any money **21** *assignment* [ə'saɪnmənt]: Auftrag **22** *charity:* Wohltätigkeits- **24** *a big slice* (AE infml): a business deal of great importance

AUSTIN: [*To* LEE] I gave him money! I already gave him money. You know that. He drank it all up!

LEE: This is a different deal here.

SAUL: We can set up a trust for your father. A large sum of money. It can be doled out to him in parcels so he can't misuse it.

AUSTIN: Yeah, and who's doing the doling?

SAUL: Your brother volunteered.

[AUSTIN *laughs.*]

LEE: That's right. I'll make sure he uses it for groceries.

AUSTIN: [*To* SAUL] I'm not doing this script! I'm not writing this crap for you or anybody else. You can't blackmail me into it. You can't threaten me into it. There's no way I'm doing it. So just give it up. Both of you.

[*Long pause.*]

SAUL: Well, that's it then. I mean this is an easy three hundred grand. Just for a first draft. It's incredible, Austin. We've got three different studios all trying to cut each other's throats to get this material. In one morning. That's how hot it is.

AUSTIN: Yeah, well you can afford to give me a percentage on the outline then. And you better get the genius here an agent before he gets burned.

LEE: Saul's gonna' be my agent. Isn't that right, Saul?

SAUL: That's right. [*To* AUSTIN] Your brother has really got something, Austin. I've been around too long not to recognize it. Raw talent.

▷ **4** *trust* (n): Vermögensverwaltung, Treuhand **5** *dole sth. out to sb.:* hand sth. out to sb. • *in parcels:* in small sums **7** *volunteer* (v): offer your services for free **10** *crap* (sl): nonsense, rubbish **11** *blackmail sb.:* jdm. erpressen **15** *grand* (n; AE sl): $ 1000 **17** *cut sb.'s throat:* do everything (including using bad and unfair means) to sb. in order to get sth.

AUSTIN: He's got a lota' balls is what he's got. He's taking you right down the river.

SAUL: Three hundred thousand, Austin. Just for a first draft. Now you've never been offered that kind of money before.

AUSTIN: I'm not writing it.

[*Pause*]

SAUL: I see. Well –

LEE: We'll just go to another writer then. Right, Saul? Just hire us somebody with some enthusiasm. Somebody who can recognize the value of a good story.

SAUL: I'm sorry about this, Austin.

AUSTIN: Yeah.

SAUL: I mean I was hoping we could continue both things but now I don't see how it's possible.

AUSTIN: So you're dropping my idea altogether. Is that it? Just trade horses in midstream? After all these months of meetings.

SAUL: I wish there was another way.

AUSTIN: I've got everything riding on this, Saul. You know that. It's my only shot. If this falls through –

SAUL: I have to go with what my instincts tell me –

AUSTIN: Your instincts!

SAUL: My gut reaction.

▷ **1** *balls* (AE sl): courage, determination **1–2** *take sb. right down the river* (infml): deceive sb. **15–16** *trade horses in midstream:* transfer your support from one person to another **18** *have everything riding on sth.:* alles auf eine Karte setzen **19** *shot* (n; infml): opportunity **22** *gut reaction:* reaction based on instinct rather than on thought and reflection

AUSTIN: You lost! That's your gut reaction. You lost a gamble. Now you're trying to tell me you like his story? How could you possibly fall for that story? It's as phony as Hopalong Cassidy. What do you see in it? I'm curious.

SAUL: It has the ring of truth, Austin.

AUSTIN: [*Laughs*] Truth?

LEE: It is true.

SAUL: Something about the real West.

AUSTIN: Why? Because it's got horses? Because it's got grown men acting like little boys?

SAUL: Something about the land. Your brother is speaking from experience.

AUSTIN: So am I!

SAUL: But nobody's interested in love these days, Austin. Let's face it.

LEE: That's right.

AUSTIN: [*To* SAUL] He's been camped out on the desert for three months. Talking to cactus. What's he know about what people wanna' see on the screen! I drive on the freeway every day. I swallow the smog. I watch the news in color. I shop in the Safeway. I'm the one who's in touch! Not him!

SAUL: I have to go now, Austin. [*He starts to leave.*]

AUSTIN: There's no such thing as the West anymore! It's a dead issue! It's dried up, Saul, and so are you.

[SAUL *stops and turns to* AUSTIN.]

SAUL: Maybe you're right. But I have to take the gamble, don't I?

▷ **3** *fall for sth.* (infml): auf etwas hereinfallen • *Hopalong Cassidy:* fictional cowboy hero, who appeared in novels, movies and TV series **5** *it has the ring of truth:* it sounds like it is essentially true **19** *swallow sth.:* etwas schlucken • *Safeway:* US supermarket chain

AUSTIN: You're a fool to do this, Saul.

SAUL: I've always gone on my hunches. Always. And I've never been wrong. [*To* LEE] I'll talk to you tomorrow, Lee.

LEE: All right, Mr Kimmer.

SAUL: Maybe we could have some lunch.

LEE: Fine with me. [*Smiles at* AUSTIN.]

SAUL: I'll give you a ring.

[SAUL *exits, lights to black as brothers look at each other from a distance.*]

▷ **2** go *on your hunches* (infml): follow your feelings and instincts

Scene Seven

Night, coyotes, crickets, sound of typewriter in dark, candlelight up on Lee *at typewriter struggling to type with one-finger system,* Austin *sits sprawled out on kitchen floor with whiskey bottle, drunk.*

Austin: [*Singing, from floor*]

Red sails in the sunset
Way out on the blue
Please carry my loved one
Home safely to me
Red sails in the sunset –

Lee: [*Slams fist on table*] Hey! Knock it off will ya'! I'm tryin' to concentrate here.

Austin: [*Laughs*] You're tryin' to concentrate?

Lee: Yeah. That's right.

Austin: Now you're tryin' to concentrate.

Lee: Between you, the coyotes and the crickets a thought don't have much of a chance.

Austin: "Between me, the coyotes and the crickets." What a great title.

Lee: I don't need a title! I need a thought.

Austin: [*Laughs*] A thought! Here's a thought for ya' –

Lee: I'm not askin' fer yer thoughts! I got my own. I can do this thing on my own.

▷ **3** *sit sprawled out:* sit in a relaxed position with your arms and legs spread out **6** *"Red sails in the sunset":* song sung by the Beatles, among others **7** *on the blue:* on the ocean/sea **11** *slam sth.:* (here) hit noisily • *knock it off* (infml): stop doing that

AUSTIN: You're going to write an entire script on your own?

LEE: That's right.

[*Pause*]

AUSTIN: Here's a thought. Saul Kimmer –

LEE: Shut up will ya'!

AUSTIN: He thinks we're the same person.

LEE: Don't get cute.

AUSTIN: He does! He's lost his mind. Poor old Saul. [*Giggles*] – Thinks we're one and the same.

LEE: Why don't you ease up on that Champagne.

AUSTIN: [*Holding up bottle*] This isn't Champagne anymore. We went through the Champagne a long time ago. This is serious stuff. The days of Champagne are long gone.

LEE: Well go outside and drink it.

AUSTIN: I'm enjoying your company, Lee. For the first time since your arrival I am finally enjoying your company. And now you want me to go outside and drink alone?

LEE: That's right. [*He reads through paper in typewriter, makes an erasure.*]

AUSTIN: You think you'll make more progress if you're alone? You might drive yourself crazy.

LEE: I could have this thing done in a night if I had a little silence.

AUSTIN: Well you'd still have the crickets to contend with. The coyotes. The sounds of the Police Helicopters prowling above the

▷ **7** *cute* (AE infml): too clever **8** *giggle:* laugh lightly in a silly or nervous way **10** *ease up on sth.:* take or do less of sth. **19** *erasure* [ɪ'reɪʒər] (fml): the removal of sth. written or printed **23** *contend with sb./sth:* have to deal with sb./sth. (that is difficult) **24** *prowl* [praʊl]: move around while looking for sth.

neighborhood. Slashing their searchlights down through the streets. Hunting for the likes of you.

LEE: I'm a screenwriter now! I'm legitimate.

AUSTIN: [*Laughing*] A screenwriter!

LEE: That's right. I'm on salary. That's more'n I can say for you. I got an advance coming.

AUSTIN: This is true. This is very true. An advance. [*Pause*] Well, maybe I oughta' go out and try my hand at your trade. Since you're doing so good at mine.

LEE: Ha! [*He attempts to type some more but gets the ribbon tangled up, starts trying to rethread it as they continue talking.*]

AUSTIN: Well why not? You don't think I've got what it takes to sneak into people's houses and steal their TVs?

LEE: You couldn't steal a toaster without losin' yer lunch.

[AUSTIN *stands with a struggle, supports himself by the sink.*]

AUSTIN: You don't think I could sneak into somebody's house and steal a toaster?

LEE: Go take a shower or somethin' will ya'! [*He gets more tangled up with the typewriter ribbon, pulling it out of the machine as though it was fishing line.*]

AUSTIN: You really don't think I could steal a crumby toaster? How much you wanna' bet I can't steal a toaster! How much? Go ahead! You're a gambler aren't you? Tell me how much yer willing

▷ **1** *slash sth.:* make violent and sweeping movements with sth. (esp. a knife) **2** *the likes of you:* people like you **3** *I'm legitimate:* (here) I have a normal and recognized job **8** *trade* (n): (here) job **10** *ribbon:* Farbband **10–11** *get sth. tangled up:* get sth. twisted and in a mess **11** *rethread sth.* [riːˈθred]: etwas entwirren **12–13** *sneak into sth.:* enter sth. (esp. a place) quietly and secretly **14** *without losing your lunch:* (here) being sick **21** *crumby* (infml): stupid, useless

to put on the line. Some part of your big advance? Oh, you haven't got that yet have you. I forgot.

LEE: All right. I'll bet you your car that you can't steal a toaster without gettin' busted.

AUSTIN: You already got my car!

LEE: Okay, your house then.

AUSTIN: What're you gonna' give me! I'm not talkin' about my house and my car, I'm talkin' about what are you gonna' give me. You don't have nothin' to give me.

LEE: I'll give you – shared screen credit. How 'bout that? I'll have it put in the contract that this was written by the both of us.

AUSTIN: I don't want my name on that piece of shit! I want something of value. You got anything of value? You got any tidbits from the desert? Any Rattlesnake bones? I'm not a greedy man. Any little personal treasure will suffice.

LEE: I'm gonna' just kick yer ass out in a minute.

AUSTIN: Oh, so now you're gonna' kick me out! Now I'm the intruder. I'm the one who's invading your precious privacy.

LEE: I'm trying to do some screenwriting here! [*He stands, picks up typewriter, slams it down hard on table. Pause, silence except for crickets.*]

AUSTIN: Well, you got everything you need. You got plenty a' coffee? Groceries. You got a car. A contract. [*Pause*] Might need a new typewriter ribbon but other than that you're pretty well fixed, I'll just leave ya' alone for a while.

▷ **1** *put sth. on the line* (AE): gamble sth., risk sth. (esp. money) **4** *get busted* (infml): be arrested **10** *shared screen credit:* Nennung beider Namen im Filmvor- bzw. -abspann **13** *tidbits* (AE): small but interesting things **15** *suffice* [sə'faɪs]: be enough **16** *kick sb.'s ass out* (sl): throw sb. out **17** *intruder:* person who is somewhere where they are not wanted; troublemaker **24** *be pretty well fixed* (infml): have everything you need

[AUSTIN *tries to steady himself to leave,* LEE *makes a move toward him.*]

LEE: Where you goin'?

AUSTIN: Don't worry about me. I'm not the one to worry about. [*He weaves toward exit, stops.*]

LEE: What're you gonna' do? Just go wander out into the night?

AUSTIN: I'm gonna' make a little tour.

LEE: Why don't ya' just go to bed for Christ's sake. Yer makin' me sick.

AUSTIN: I can take care a' myself. Don't worry about me.

[AUSTIN *weaves badly in another attempt to exit, he crashes to the floor,* LEE *goes to him but remains standing.*]

LEE: You want me to call your wife for ya' or something?

AUSTIN: [*From floor*] My wife?

LEE: Yeah. I mean maybe she can help ya' out. Talk to ya' or somethin'.

AUSTIN: [*Struggles to stand up again*] She's five hundred miles away. North. North of here. Up in the north country where things are calm. I don't need any help. I'm gonna' go outside and I'm gonna' steal a toaster. I'm gonna' steal some other stuff too. I might even commit bigger crimes. Bigger than you ever dreamed of. Crimes beyond the imagination!

[AUSTIN *manages to get himself vertical, tries to head for exit again.*]

LEE: Just hang on a minute, AUSTIN.

AUSTIN: Why? What for? You don't need my help, right? You got a handle on the project. Besides, I'm lookin' forward to the smell of

▷ **1** *steady yourself:* stop yourself from falling or shaking **5** *weave:* move forward in an irregular way **24** *hang on a minute:* wait a minute **25–26** *get a handle on sth.* (infml): understand how to do sth.

the night. The bushes. Orange blossoms. Dust in the driveways. Rain bird sprinklers. Lights in people's houses. You're right about the lights, Lee. Everybody else is livin' the life. Indoors. Safe. This is a Paradise down here. You know that? We're livin' in a Paradise. We've forgotten about that.

LEE: You sound just like the old man now.

AUSTIN: Yeah, well we all sound alike when we're sloshed. We just sorta' echo each other.

LEE: Maybe if we could work on this together we could bring him back out here. Get him settled down some place.

[AUSTIN *turns violently toward* LEE, *takes a swing at him, misses and crashes to the floor again.* LEE *stays standing.*]

AUSTIN: I don't want him out here! I've had it with him! I went all the way out there! I went out of my way. I gave him money and all he did was play Al Jolson records and spit at me! I gave him money!

[*Pause*]

LEE: Just help me a little with the characters, all right? You know how to do it, Austin.

AUSTIN: [*On floor, laughs*] The characters!

LEE: Yeah. You know. The way they talk and stuff. I can hear it in my head but I can't get it down on paper.

AUSTIN: What characters?

LEE: The guys. The guys in the story.

AUSTIN: Those aren't characters.

LEE: Whatever you call 'em then. I need to write somethin' out.

▷ **2** *rain bird sprinkler:* Rasensprenger **7** *sloshed* [slɑːʃt] (adj; infml): drunk **11** *take a swing at sb.* (infml): aim a blow at sb. **13** *I've had it with him* (sl): I am fed up with him **14** *I went out of my way:* I took particular care and trouble **15** *Al Jolson* (1886–1950): US singer and comedian

AUSTIN: Those are illusions of characters.

LEE: I don't give a damn what ya' call 'em! You know what I'm talkin' about!

AUSTIN: Those are fantasies of a long lost boyhood.

LEE: I gotta' write somethin' out on paper!

[*Pause*]

AUSTIN: What for? Saul's gonna' get you a fancy screenwriter isn't he?

LEE: I wanna' do it myself!

AUSTIN: Then do it! Yer on your own now old buddy. You bulldogged yer way into contention. Now you gotta' carry it through.

LEE: I will but I need some advice. Just a couple a' things. Come on, Austin. Just help me get 'em talkin' right. It won't take much.

AUSTIN: Oh, now you're having a little doubt, huh? What happened? The pressure's on, boy. This is it. You gotta' come up with it now. You don't come up with a winner on your first time out they just cut your head off. They don't give you a second chance ya' know.

LEE: I got a good story! I know it's a good story. I just need a little help is all.

AUSTIN: Not from me. Not from yer little old brother. I'm retired.

LEE: You could save this thing for me, Austin. I'd give ya' half the money. I would. I only need half anyway. With this kinda' money I could be a long time down the road. I'd never bother ya' again. I promise. You'd never even see me again.

AUSTIN: [*Still on floor*] You'd disappear?

LEE: I would for sure.

▷ **2** *I don't give a damn* (infml): I don't care at all **9–10** *bulldog your way into contention:* push your way forward into a position regardless of other people's feelings or interests **14** *the pressure is on* (infml): (here) now you really have to work hard • *come up with sth.:* etwas vorweisen/präsentieren

AUSTIN: Where would you disappear to?

LEE: That don't matter. I got plenty a' places.

AUSTIN: Nobody can disappear. The old man tried that. Look where it got him. He lost his teeth.

LEE: He never had any money.

AUSTIN: I don't mean that. I mean his teeth! His real teeth. First he lost his real teeth, then he lost his false teeth. You never knew that did ya'? He never confided in you.

LEE: Nah, I never knew that.

AUSTIN: You wanna' drink?

[AUSTIN *offers bottle to* LEE, LEE *takes it, sits down on kitchen floor with* AUSTIN, *they share the bottle.*]

Yeah, he lost his real teeth one at a time. Woke up every morning with another tooth lying on the mattress. Finally, he decides he's gotta' get 'em all pulled out but he doesn't have any money. Middle of Arizona with no money and no insurance and every morning another tooth is lying on the mattress. [*Takes a drink.*] So what does he do?

LEE: I dunno'. I never knew about that.

AUSTIN: He begs the government. G.I. Bill or some damn thing. Some pension plan he remembers in the back of his head. And they send him out the money.

LEE: They did?

[*They keep trading the bottle between them taking drinks.*]

▷ **8** *confide in sb.:* tell sb. sth. that is very personal **14** *mattress:* Matratze **16** *insurance:* (hier) Krankenversicherung **20** *G.I. Bill:* bill (1944) which provided federal aid to veterans of World War II and later military conflicts (*G.I.:* US army soldier) **24** *trade sth.:* (here) exchange sth., take turns sharing sth.

AUSTIN: Yeah. They send him the money but it's not enough money. Costs a lot to have all yer teeth yanked. They charge by the individual tooth, ya' know. I mean one tooth isn't equal to another tooth. Some are more expensive. Like the big ones in the back –

LEE: So what happened?

AUSTIN: So he locates a Mexican dentist in Juarez who'll do the whole thing for a song. And he takes off hitchhiking to the border.

LEE: Hitchhiking?

AUSTIN: Yeah. So how long you think it takes him to get to the border? A man his age.

LEE: I dunno'.

AUSTIN: Eight days it takes him. Eight days in the rain and the sun and every day he's droppin' teeth on the blacktop and nobody'll pick him up 'cause his mouth's full a' blood.

[*Pause, they drink.*]

So finally he stumbles into the dentist. Dentist takes all his money and all his teeth. And there he is, in Mexico, with his gums sewed up and his pockets empty.

[*Long silence,* AUSTIN *drinks.*]

LEE: That's it?

AUSTIN: Then I go out to see him, see. I go out there and I take him out for a nice Chinese dinner. But he doesn't eat. All he wants to do is drink Martinis outa' plastic cups. And he takes his teeth out and lays 'em on the table 'cause he can't stand the feel of 'em. And we ask the waitress for one a' those doggie bags to take the Chop Suey

▷ **2** *yank sth.* (infml): pull sth. with a sudden sharp movement **6** *locate sb.:* (here) find sb. • *Juarez:* Mexican city on the border with the USA **7** *for a song* (infml): very cheaply **13** *blacktop* (AE): asphalt used for the surface of a road **16** *stumble into sth.:* walk into sth. with no energy **17–18** *with his gums sewed up* [soʊd]: mit zahnlosem Mund **25** *doggie bag* (AE): bag offered by restaurants to take food home (originally for pets) • *Chop Suey* [tʃɑːp 'suːi]: Chinese meal

home in. So he drops his teeth in the doggie bag along with the Chop Suey. And then we go out to hit all the bars up and down the highway. Says he wants to introduce me to all his buddies. And in one a' those bars, in one a' those bars up and down the highway, he left that doggie bag with his teeth lying in the Chop Suey.

LEE: You never found it?

AUSTIN: We went back but we never did find it. [*Pause*] Now that's a true story. True to life.

[*They drink as lights fade to black.*]

▷ **2** *hit all the bars* (infml): go from one bar to another

SCENE EIGHT

Very early morning, between night and day, no crickets, coyotes yapping feverishly in distance before light comes up. A small fire blazes up in the dark from alcove area, sound of LEE *smashing typewriter with a golf club, lights coming up,* LEE *seen smashing typewriter methodically then dropping pages of his script into a burning bowl set on the floor of alcove, flames leap up.* AUSTIN *has a whole bunch of stolen toasters lined up on the sink counter along with Lee's stolen TV. The toasters are of a wide variety of models, mostly chrome,* AUSTIN *goes up and down the line of toasters, breathing on them and polishing them with a dish towel. Both men are drunk, empty whiskey bottles and beer cans litter floor of kitchen, they share a half-empty bottle on one of the chairs in the alcove,* LEE *keeps periodically taking deliberate ax-chops at the typewriter, using a nine-iron as* AUSTIN *speaks, all of their mother's house plants are dead and drooping.*

AUSTIN: [*Polishing toasters*] There's gonna' be a general lack of toast in the neighborhood this morning. Many, many unhappy, bewildered breakfast faces. I guess it's best not to even think of the victims. Not to even entertain it. Is that the right psychology?

LEE: [*Pause*] What?

AUSTIN: Is that the correct criminal psychology? Not to think of the victims?

LEE: What victims? [*He takes another swipe at typewriter with nine-iron, adds pages to the fire.*]

▷ **3** *blaze up:* burst into flames **11** *litter sth.:* lie around sth. in a mess **13** *deliberate:* intentional; done on purpose • *take ax-chops:* hit hard as if cutting wood with an ax **14** *nine-iron:* kind of golf club **15** *droop:* hang down **17–18** *bewildered* (adj): confused, surprised **19** *entertain sth.:* allow yourself to think about sth. **23** *take a swipe:* hit sth. with a quick swinging blow

AUSTIN: The victims of crime. Of breaking and entering. I mean is it a prerequisite for a criminal not to have a conscience?

LEE: Ask a criminal. [*Pause.* LEE *stares at* AUSTIN.] What're you gonna' do with all those toasters? That's the dumbest thing I ever saw in my life.

AUSTIN: I've got hundreds of dollars' worth of household appliances here. You may not realize that.

LEE: Yeah, and how many hundreds of dollars did you walk right past?

AUSTIN: It was toasters you challenged me to. Only toasters. I ignored every other temptation.

LEE: I never challenged you! That's no challenge. Anybody can steal a toaster.

[*He smashes typewriter again.*]

AUSTIN: You don't have to take it out on my typewriter ya' know. It's not the machine's fault that you can't write. It's a sin to do that to a good machine.

LEE: A sin?

AUSTIN: When you consider all the writers who never even had a machine. Who would have given an eyeball for a good typewriter. Any typewriter.

[LEE *smashes typewriter again.*]

[*Polishing toaster.*] All the ones who wrote on matchbook covers. Paper bags. Toilet paper. Who had their writing destroyed by their

▷ **1** *breaking and entering:* Einbruch **2** *prerequisite* [priːˈrekwəzɪt] (n): necessary pre-condition • *conscience:* Gewissen **6** *household appliance* [əˈplaɪəns]: machine that is designed to do a particular thing in the home **10** *challenge sb. to do sth.:* invite sb. to do sth., e.g. to see who is better at it **11** *temptation:* Versuchung **15** *take it out on sth.:* seine Wut an etwas auslassen **16** *sin:* Sünde

jailers. Who persisted beyond all odds. Those writers would find it hard to understand your actions.

[LEE *comes down on typewriter with one final crushing blow of the nine-iron then collapses in one of the chairs, takes a drink from bottle. Pause*]

[*After pause.*] Not to mention demolishing a perfectly good golf club. What about all the struggling golfers? What about Lee Trevino? What do you think he would've said when he was batting balls around with broomsticks at the age of nine. Impoverished.

[*Pause*]

LEE: What time is it anyway?

AUSTIN: No idea. Time stands still when you're havin' fun.

LEE: Is it too late to call a woman? You know any women?

AUSTIN: I'm a married man.

LEE: I mean a local woman.

[AUSTIN *looks out at light through window above sink.*]

AUSTIN: It's either too late or too early. You're the nature enthusiast. Can't you tell the time by the light in the sky? Orient yourself around the North Star or something?

LEE: I can't tell anything.

AUSTIN: Maybe you need a little breakfast. Some toast! How 'bout some toast?

[AUSTIN *goes to cupboard, pulls out loaf of bread and starts dropping slices into every toaster,* LEE *stays sitting, drinks, watches* AUSTIN.]

▷ **1** *jailer:* person in charge of a prison or working in a prison to maintain order • *persist beyond all odds:* not give up in spite of many difficulties **7–8** *Lee Trevino* (born 1939): US American golfer of Mexican descent **8** *bat sth.:* hit sth. with a club **9** *broomstick:* Besenstiel • *impoverished:* (here) living in poverty

LEE: I don't need toast. I need a woman.

AUSTIN: A woman isn't the answer. Never was.

LEE: I'm not talkin' about permanent. I'm talkin' about temporary.

AUSTIN: [*Putting toast in toasters*] We'll just test the merits of these little demons. See which brands have a tendency to burn. See which one can produce a perfectly golden piece of fluffy toast.

LEE: How much gas you got in yer car?

AUSTIN: I haven't driven my car for days now. So I haven't had an opportunity to look at the gas gauge.

LEE: Take a guess. You think there's enough to get me to Bakersfield?

AUSTIN: Bakersfield? What's in Bakersfield?

LEE: Just never mind what's in Bakersfield! You think there's enough goddamn gas in the car!

AUSTIN: Sure.

LEE: Sure. You could care less, right. Let me run outa' gas on the Grapevine. You could give a shit.

AUSTIN: I'd say there was enough gas to get you just about anywhere, Lee. With your determination and guts.

LEE: What the hell time is it anyway?

[LEE *pulls out his wallet, starts going through dozens of small pieces of paper, with phone numbers written on them, drops some on the floor, drops others in the fire.*]

▷ **4** *merit:* (here) quality **5** *brand:* Marke **6** *fluffy:* (here) soft and light **9** *gas gauge* [geɪdʒ]: instrument for measuring the amount of gas in a car's tank **10** *Bakersfield:* city in southern California **15** *could care less = couldn't care less:* not be at all interested **15–16** *the Grapevine:* road from Los Angeles to Bakersfield which crosses a mountain range **16** *could give a shit = couldn't give a shit* (sl): be completely indifferent and unconcerned **18** *guts* (pl; infml): courage

AUSTIN: Very early. This is the time of morning when the coyotes kill people's cocker spaniels. Did you hear them? That's what they were doing out there. Luring innocent pets away from their homes.

LEE: [*Searching through his papers*] What's the area code for Bakersfield? You know?

AUSTIN: You could always call the operator.

LEE: I can't stand that voice they give ya'.

AUSTIN: What voice?

LEE: That voice that warns you that if you'd only tried harder to find the number in the phone book you wouldn't have to be calling the operator to begin with. [*He gets up, holding a slip of paper from his wallet, stumbles toward phone on wall, yanks receiver, starts dialing.*]

AUSTIN: Well I don't understand why you'd want to talk to anybody else anyway. I mean you can talk to me. I'm your brother.

LEE: [*Dialing*] I wanna' talk to a woman. I haven't heard a woman's voice in a long time.

AUSTIN: Not since the Botanist?

LEE: What?

AUSTIN: Nothing. [*Starts singing as he tends toast.*]

Red sails in the sunset
Way out on the blue
Please carry my loved one
Home safely to me.

LEE: Hey, knock it off will ya'! This is long distance here.

AUSTIN: Bakersfield?

▷ **3** *lure sb.:* persuade or trick sb. to go somewhere **6** *operator:* Telefonist(in), Vermittlung **7** *I can't stand sth.:* I dislike sth. strongly **11** *to begin with:* in the first place **13** *dial* ['daɪəl]: push buttons to call a telephone number **20** *tend sth.:* take care of sth. **25** *knock it off* (infml): stop that • *long distance:* Ferngespräch

LEE: Yeah, Bakersfield. It's Kern County.

AUSTIN: Well, what County are *we* in?

LEE: You better get yerself a 7-Up, boy.

AUSTIN: One County's as good as another.

[AUSTIN *hums "Red Sails" softly as* LEE *talks on phone.*]

LEE: [*To phone*] Yeah, operator, look – first off I wanna' know the area code for Bakersfield. Right. Bakersfield! Okay. Good. Now I wanna' know if you can help me track somebody down. [*Pause.*] No, no I mean a phone number. Just a phone number. Okay. [*Holds piece of paper up and reads it*] Okay, the name is Melly Ferguson. Melly. [*Pause.*] I dunno'. Melly. Maybe. Yeah. Maybe Melanie. Yeah. Melanie Ferguson. Okay. [*Pause.*] What? I can't hear ya' so good. Sounds like yer under the ocean. [*Pause.*] You got ten Melanie Fergusons? How could that be? Ten Melanie Fergusons in Bakersfield? Well gimme all of 'em then. [*Pause.*] What d'ya' mean? Gimme all ten Melanie Fergusons! That's right. Just a second. [*To* AUSTIN] Gimme a pen.

AUSTIN: I don't have a pen.

LEE: Gimme a pencil then!

AUSTIN: I don't have a pencil.

LEE: [*To phone*] Just a second, operator. [*To* AUSTIN] Yer a writer and ya' don't have a pen or a pencil!

AUSTIN: I'm not a writer. You're a writer.

LEE: I'm on the phone here! Get me a pen or a pencil.

AUSTIN: I gotta' watch the toast.

▷ **1** *Kern County:* county (= Landkreis) north of Los Angeles **5** *hum:* sing with your lips closed **8** *track sb. down:* find out where sb. is

LEE: [*To phone*] Hang on a second, operator. [LEE *lets the phone drop then starts pulling all the drawers in the kitchen out on the floor and dumping the contents, searching for a pencil,* AUSTIN *watches him casually. Crashing through drawers, throwing contents around kitchen*] This is the last time I try to live with people, boy! I can't believe it. Here I am! Here I am again in a desperate situation! This would never happen out on the desert. I would never be in this kinda' situation out on the desert. Isn't there a pen or pencil in this house! Who lives in this house anyway!

AUSTIN: Our mother.

LEE: How come she don't have a pen or a pencil! She's a social person isn't she? Doesn't she have to make shopping lists? She's gotta' have a pencil. [*Finds a pencil.*] Aaha! [*He rushes back to phone, picks up receiver.*] All right, operator. Operator? Hey! Operator! Goddamnit! [*He rips the phone off the wall and throws it down, goes back to chair and falls into it, drinks. Long pause.*]

AUSTIN: She hung up?

LEE: Yeah, she hung up. I knew she was gonna' hang up. I could hear it in her voice. [*He starts going through his slips of paper again.*]

AUSTIN: Well, you're probably better off staying here with me anyway. I'll take care of you.

LEE: I don't need takin' care of! Not by you anyway.

AUSTIN: Toast is almost ready. [*He starts buttering all the toast as it pops up.*]

LEE: I don't want any toast!

[*Long pause*]

AUSTIN: You gotta' eat something. Can't just drink. How long have we been drinking, anyway?

▷ **2** *drawer:* Schublade **3** *dump sth.:* drop sth. in a careless way **15** *Goddamnit* (infml): God damn it • *rip sth.:* tear/pull sth. with force

Lee: [*Looking through slips of paper*] Maybe it was Fresno. What's the area code for Fresno? How could I have lost that number! She was beautiful.

[*Pause*]

Austin: Why don't you just forget about that, Lee. Forget about the woman.

Lee: She had green eyes. You know what green eyes do to me?

Austin: I know but you're not gonna' get it on with her now anyway. It's dawn already. She's in Bakersfield for Christ's sake.

[*Long pause,* Lee *considers the situation.*]

Lee: Yeah. [*Looks at windows*] It's dawn!

Austin: Let's just have some toast and –

Lee: What is this bullshit with the toast anyway! You make it sound like salvation or something. I don't want any goddamn toast! How many times I gotta' tell ya'!

[Lee *gets up, crosses up stage to windows in alcove, looks out.* Austin *butters toast.*]

Austin: Well it is like salvation sort of. I mean the smell. I love the smell of toast. And the sun's coming up. It makes me feel like anything's possible. Ya' know?

Lee: [*Back to* Austin, *facing windows up stage*] So go to church why don't ya'.

Austin: Like a beginning. I love beginnings.

Lee: Oh yeah. I've always been kinda' partial to endings myself.

Austin: What if I come with you, Lee?

▷ **1** *Fresno:* city in central California **9** *dawn:* the early morning when the first light appears **14** *salvation:* Erlösung **21–22** *why don't ya* (sl): used in a derogatory manner to ask a question (here: "Why don't you go to church then?") **24** *be partial to sth.:* like sth., be fond of sth.

LEE: [*Pause as* LEE *turns toward* AUSTIN] What?

AUSTIN: What if I come with you out to the desert?

LEE: Are you kiddin'?

AUSTIN: No. I'd just like to see what it's like.

LEE: You wouldn't last a day out there pal.

AUSTIN: That's what you said about the toasters. You said I couldn't steal a toaster either.

LEE: A toaster's got nothin' to do with the desert.

AUSTIN: I could make it, Lee. I'm not that helpless. I can cook.

LEE: Cook?

AUSTIN: I can.

LEE: So what! You can cook. Toast.

AUSTIN: I can make fires. I know how to get fresh water from condensation.

[AUSTIN *stacks buttered toast up in a tall stack on plate.* LEE *slams table.*]

LEE: It's not somethin' you learn out of a Boy Scout Handbook!

AUSTIN: Well how do you learn it then! How're you supposed to learn it!

[*Pause*]

LEE: Ya' just learn it, that's all. Ya' learn it 'cause ya' have to learn it. You don't *have* to learn it.

AUSTIN: You could teach me.

LEE: [*Stands*] What're you, crazy or somethin'? You went to college. Here, you are down here, rollin' in bucks. Floatin' up and down in elevators. And you wanna' learn how to live on the desert!

▷ **15** *stack sth. up:* put sth. in a pile one on top of the other **24** *be rolling in bucks* (sl): have a lot of money (*buck:* dollar) • *float up and down:* move up and down

AUSTIN: I do, Lee. I really do. There's nothin' down here for me. There never was. When we were kids here it was different. There was a life here then. But now – I keep comin' down here thinkin' it's the fifties or somethin'. I keep finding myself getting off the freeway at familiar landmarks that turn out to be unfamiliar. On the way to appointments. Wandering down streets I thought I recognized that turn out to be replicas of streets I remember. Streets I misremember. Streets I can't tell if I lived on or saw in a postcard. Fields that don't even exist anymore.

LEE: There's no point cryin' about that now.

AUSTIN: There's nothin' real down here, Lee! Least of all me!

LEE: Well I can't save you from that!

AUSTIN: You could let me come with you.

LEE: No dice, pal.

AUSTIN: You could let me come with you, Lee!

LEE: Hey, do you actually think I chose to live out in the middle a' nowhere? Do ya'? Ya' think it's some kinda' philosophical decision I took or somethin'? I'm livin' out there 'cause I can't make it here! And yer bitchin' to me about all yer success!

AUSTIN: I'd cash it all in in a second. That's the truth.

LEE: [*Pause, shakes his head*] I can't believe this.

AUSTIN: Let me go with you.

LEE: Stop sayin' that will ya'! Yer worse than a dog.

[AUSTIN *offers out the plate of neatly stacked toast to* LEE.]

AUSTIN: You want some toast?

▷ **4** *fifties:* 1950s **7** *replica* ['replɪkə]: copy, reproduction **14** *no dice* (AE sl): kommt nicht in Frage **19** *bitch about sth.* (AE sl): criticize sth., complain about sth. **20** *cash sth. in:* exchange sth. for another thing

[LEE *suddenly explodes and knocks the plate out of* AUSTIN'*s hand, toast goes flying. Long frozen moment where it appears* LEE *might go all the way this time when* AUSTIN *breaks it by slowly lowering himself to his knees and begins gathering the scattered toast from the floor and stacking it back on the plate.* LEE *begins to circle* AUSTIN *in a slow, predatory way, crushing pieces of toast in his wake, no words for a while.* AUSTIN *keeps gathering toast, even the crushed pieces.*]

LEE: Tell ya' what I'll do little brother. I might just consider makin' you a deal. Little trade.

[AUSTIN *continues gathering toast as* LEE *circles him through this.*]

You write me up this screenplay thing just like I tell ya'. I mean you can use all yer usual tricks and stuff. Yer fancy language. Yer artistic hocus pocus. But ya' gotta' write everything like I say. Every move. Every time they run outa' gas, they run outa' gas. Every time they wanna' jump on a horse, they do just that. If they wanna' stay in Texas, by God they'll stay in Texas! [*Keeps circling.*] And you finish the whole thing up for me. Top to bottom. And you put my name on it. And I own all the rights. And every dime goes in my pocket. You do all that and I'll sure enough take ya' with me to the desert. [LEE *stops, pause, looks down at* AUSTIN.] How's that sound?

[*Pause as* AUSTIN *stands slowly, holding plate of demolished toast. Their faces are very close, pause.*]

AUSTIN: It's a deal.

[LEE *stares straight into* AUSTIN'*s eyes, then he slowly takes a piece of toast off the plate, raises it to his mouth and takes a huge crushing bite, never taking his eyes off* AUSTIN'*s. As* LEE *crunches into the toast the lights black out.*]

▷ **6** *predatory* ['predətɔːri]: like an animal that lives by hunting other animals for food **6–7** *in his wake:* (here) as he walks; behind him **14** *hocus pocus* [ˌhoʊkəs 'poʊkəs]: nonsense; unreal magic **19** *dime* (AE): US coin worth 10 cents **28** *crunch into sth.:* bite sth.

Mid-day, no sound, blazing heat, the stage is ravaged; bottles, toasters, smashed typewriter, ripped out telephone, etc. All the debris from previous scene is now starkly visible in intense yellow light; the effect should be like a desert junkyard at high noon, the coolness of the preceding scenes is totally obliterated. AUSTIN *is seated at table in alcove, shirt open, pouring with sweat, hunched over a writing notebook, scribbling notes desperately with a ball-point pen.* LEE *with no shirt, beer in hand, sweat pouring down his chest, is walking a slow circle around the table, picking his way through the objects, sometimes kicking them aside.*

LEE: [*As he walks*] All right, read it back to me. Read it back to me!

AUSTIN: [*Scribbling at top speed*] Just a second.

LEE: Come on, come on! Just read what ya' got.

AUSTIN: I can't keep up! It's not the same as if I had a typewriter.

LEE: Just read what we got so far. Forget about the rest.

AUSTIN: All right. Let's see – okay – [AUSTIN *wipes sweat from his face, reads as* LEE *circles.*] Luke says uh –

LEE: Luke?

AUSTIN: Yeah.

LEE: His name's Luke? All right, all right – we can change the names later. What's he say? Come on, come on.

AUSTIN: He says uh – [*Reading*] "I told ya' you were a fool to follow me in here. I know this prairie like the back a' my hand."

▷ **1** *ravaged:* in a complete mess, badly damaged **3** *debris* [də'bri:]: Trümmer **4** *junkyard:* Schrottplatz **5** *obliterate sth.* [ə'blɪtəreɪt]: wipe sth. out; remove all traces of sth. **7** *scribble sth.:* write sth. quickly and carelessly **23** *know sth. like the back of your hand:* etwas in- und auswendig kennen

LEE: No, no, no! That's not what I said. I never said that.

AUSTIN: That's what I wrote.

LEE: It's not what I said. I never said "like the back a' my hand". That's stupid. That's one a' those – whadya' call it? Whadya' call that?

AUSTIN: What?

LEE: Whadya' call it when somethin's been said a thousand times before. Whadya' call that?

AUSTIN: Um – a cliché?

LEE: Yeah. That's right. Cliché. That's what that is. A cliché. "The back a' my hand." That's stupid.

AUSTIN: That's what you said.

LEE: I never said that! And even if I did, that's where yer supposed to come in. That's where yer supposed to change it to somethin' better.

AUSTIN: Well how am I supposed to do that and write down what you say at the same time?

LEE: Ya' just do, that's all! You hear a stupid line you change it. That's yer job.

AUSTIN: All right. [*Makes more notes.*]

LEE: What're you changin' it to?

AUSTIN: I'm not changing it. I'm just trying to catch up.

LEE: Well change it! We gotta' change that, we can't leave that in there like that. "… the back a' my hand." That's dumb.

AUSTIN: [*Stops writing, sits back*] All right.

LEE: [*Pacing*] So what'll we change it to?

AUSTIN: Um – How 'bout – "I'm on intimate terms with this prairie."

▷ **26** *be on intimate terms with sb./sth.:* have an intimate relationship with sb./sth.

LEE: [*To himself, considering line as he walks*] "I'm on intimate terms with this prairie." Intimate terms, intimate terms. Intimate – that means like uh – sexual, right?

AUSTIN: Well – yeah – or –

LEE: He's on sexual terms with the prairie? How dya' figure that?

AUSTIN: Well it doesn't necessarily have to mean sexual.

LEE: What's it mean then?

AUSTIN: It means uh – close – personal –

LEE: All right. How's it sound? Put it into the uh – the line there. Read it back. Let's see how it sounds. [*To himself*] "Intimate terms."

AUSTIN: [*Scribbles in notebook*] Okay. It'd go something like this: [*Reads*] "I told ya' you were a fool to follow me in here. I'm on intimate terms with this prairie."

LEE: That's good. I like that. That's real good.

AUSTIN: You do?

LEE: Yeah. Don't you?

AUSTIN: Sure.

LEE: Sounds original now. "Intimate terms." That's good. Okay. Now we're cookin'! That has a real ring to it.

[AUSTIN *makes more notes,* LEE *walks around, pours beer on his arms and rubs it over his chest feeling good about the new progress. As he does this* MOM *enters unobtrusively down stage left with her luggage. She stops and stares at the scene, still holding luggage, as the two men continue, unaware of her presence,* AUSTIN *absorbed in his writing,* LEE *cooling himself off with beer.* LEE *continues.*]

▷ **5** *figure sth.* (AE infml): think that sth. is true; decide sth. **19** *be cooking* (AE sl): be filled with enthusiasm; be doing well • *ring:* resonance **22** *unobtrusively* [ˌʌnəb'truːsɪvli]: without being noticed **24** *absorbed:* concentrating so hard on sth. that you ignore other things

Lee: "He's on intimate terms with this prairie." Sounds real mysterious and kinda' threatening at the same time.

Austin: [*Writing rapidly*] Good.

Lee: Now –

[Lee *turns and suddenly sees* Mom, *he stares at her for a while, she stares back,* Austin *keeps writing feverishly, not noticing.* Lee *walks slowly over to* Mom *and takes a closer look. Long pause.*]

Mom?

[Austin *looks up suddenly from his writing, sees* Mom, *stands quickly, long pause.* Mom *surveys the damage.*]

Austin: Mom. What're you doing back?

Mom: I'm back.

Lee: Here, lemme take those for ya'.

[Lee *sets beer on counter then takes both her bags, but doesn't know where to set them down in the sea of junk so he just keeps holding them.*]

Austin: I wasn't expecting you back so soon. I thought uh – How was Alaska?

Mom: Fine.

Lee: See any igloos?

Mom: No. Just glaciers.

Austin: Cold, huh?

Mom: What?

Austin: It must've been cold up there?

Mom: Not really.

▷ **21** *glacier* ['gleɪʃər]: Gletscher

LEE: Musta' been colder than this here. I mean we're havin' a real scorcher here.

MOM: Oh? [*She looks at damage.*]

LEE: Yeah. Must be in the hundreds.

AUSTIN: You wanna' take your coat off, Mom?

MOM: No. [*Pause, she surveys space.*] What happened in here?

AUSTIN: Oh um – Me and Lee were just sort of celebrating and uh –

MOM: Celebrating?

AUSTIN: Yeah. Uh – Lee sold a screenplay. A story, I mean.

MOM: Lee did?

AUSTIN: Yeah.

MOM: Not you?

AUSTIN: No. Him.

MOM: [*To* LEE] You sold a screenplay?

LEE: Yeah. That's right. We're just sorta' finishing it up right now. That's what we're doing here.

AUSTIN: Me and Lee are going out to the desert to live.

MOM: You and Lee?

AUSTIN: Yeah. I'm taking off with Lee.

MOM: [*She looks back and forth at each of them. Pause.*] You gonna' go live with your father?

AUSTIN: No. We're going to a different desert, Mom.

MOM: I see. Well, you'll probably wind up on the same desert sooner or later. What're all these toasters doing here?

▷ **2** *scorcher* (n; infml): extremely hot day **4** *be in the hundreds:* more than 100 degrees Fahrenheit (ca. 40 °C) **19** *take off* (infml): leave (everything behind)

AUSTIN: Well – we had a kind of contest.

MOM: Contest?

LEE: Yeah.

AUSTIN: Lee won.

MOM: Did you win a lot of money, Lee?

LEE: Well, not yet. It's comin' in any day now.

MOM: [*To* LEE] What happened to your shirt?

LEE: Oh. I was sweatin' like a pig and I took it off.

[AUSTIN *grabs* LEE'*s shirt off the table and tosses it to him.* LEE *sets down suitcases and puts his shirt on.*]

MOM: Well it's one hell of a mess in here isn't it?

AUSTIN: Yeah, I'll clean it up for you, Mom. I just didn't know you were coming back so soon.

MOM: I didn't either.

AUSTIN: What happened?

MOM: Nothing. I just started missing all my plants. [*She notices dead plants.*]

AUSTIN: Oh.

MOM: Oh, they're all dead aren't they. [*She crosses toward them, examines them closely.*] You didn't get a chance to water, I guess.

AUSTIN: I was doing it and then Lee came and –

LEE: Yeah I just distracted him a whole lot here, Mom. It's not his fault.

[*Pause, as* MOM *stares at plants.*]

▷ **1** *contest:* competition **22** *distract sb.:* take sb.'s attention away

MOM: Oh well, one less thing to take care of I guess. [*Turns toward brothers.*] Oh, that reminds me – You boys will probably never guess who's in town. Try and guess.

[*Long pause, brothers stare at her.*]

AUSTIN: Whadya' mean, Mom?

MOM: Take a guess. Somebody very important has come to town. I read it, coming down on the Greyhound.

LEE: Somebody very important?

MOM: See if you can guess. You'll never guess.

AUSTIN: Mom – we're trying to uh – [*Points to writing pad.*]

MOM: Picasso. [*Pause.*] Picasso's in town. Isn't that incredible? Right now.

[*Pause*]

AUSTIN: Picasso's dead, Mom.

MOM: No, he's not dead. He's visiting the museum. I read it on the bus. We have to go down there and see him.

AUSTIN: Mom –

MOM: This is the chance of a lifetime. Can you imagine? We could all go down and meet him. All three of us.

LEE: Uh – I don't think I'm really up fer meetin' anybody right now. I'm uh – What's his name?

MOM: Picasso! Picasso! You've never heard of Picasso? Austin, you've heard of Picasso.

AUSTIN: Mom, we're not going to have time.

▷ **7** *Greyhound:* long-distance US bus line **10** *writing pad:* Schreibblock **11** *Picasso = Pablo Picasso* (1881–1973): Spanish painter and sculptor, one of the most influential artists of the 20th century **20** *be up for sth.:* (infml) mentally prepared to take part in sth., want to do sth.

MOM: It won't take long. We'll just hop in the car and go down there. An opportunity like this doesn't come along every day.

AUSTIN: We're gonna' be leavin' here, Mom!

[*Pause*]

MOM: Oh.

LEE: Yeah.

[*Pause*]

MOM: You're both leaving?

LEE: [*Looks at* AUSTIN] Well we were thinkin' about that before but now I –

AUSTIN: No, we are! We're both leaving. We've got it all planned.

MOM: [*To* AUSTIN] Well you can't leave. You have a family.

AUSTIN: I'm leaving. I'm getting out of here.

LEE: [*To* MOM] I don't really think Austin's cut out for the desert, do you?

MOM: No. He's not.

AUSTIN: I'm going with you, Lee!

MOM: He's too thin.

LEE: Yeah, he'd just burn up out there.

AUSTIN: [*To* LEE] We just gotta' finish this screenplay and then we're gonna' take off. That's the plan. That's what you said. Come on, let's get back to work, Lee.

LEE: I can't work under these conditions here. It's too hot.

AUSTIN: Then we'll do it on the desert.

LEE: Don't be tellin' me what we're gonna' do!

▷ **14** *be cut out for sth.* (infml): have the qualities needed for sth.

MOM: Don't shout in the house.

LEE: We're just gonna' have to postpone the whole deal.

AUSTIN: I can't postpone it! It's gone past postponing! I'm doing everything you said. I'm writing down exactly what you tell me.

LEE: Yeah, but you were right all along see. It is a dumb story. "Two lamebrains chasin' each other across Texas." That's what you said, right?

AUSTIN: I never said that.

[LEE *sneers in* AUSTIN'*s* face, *then turns to* MOM.]

LEE: I'm gonna' just borrow some a' your antiques, Mom. You don't mind do ya'? Just a few plates and things. Silverware.

[LEE *starts going through all the cupboards in the kitchen, pulling out plates and stacking them on counter as* MOM *and* AUSTIN *watch.*]

MOM: You don't have any utensils on the desert?

LEE: Nah, I'm fresh out.

AUSTIN: [*To* LEE] What're you doing?

MOM: Well some of those are very old. Bone china.

LEE: I'm tired of eatin' outa' my bare hands, ya' know. It's not civilized.

AUSTIN: [*To* LEE] What're you doing? We made a deal!

MOM: Couldn't you borrow the plastic ones instead? I have plenty of plastic ones.

LEE: [*As he stacks plates*] It's not the same. Plastic's not the same at all. What I need is somethin' authentic. Somethin' to

▷ **2** *postpone sth.:* etwas aufschieben **9** *sneer:* smile in an unpleasant way that shows you do not respect sb. **16** *I'm fresh out (of sth.)* (AE infml): I no longer have sth. **18** *bone china:* very fine porcelain

keep me in touch. It's easy to get outa' touch out there. Don't worry I'll get 'em back to ya'.

[AUSTIN *rushes up to* LEE, *grabs him by shoulders*.]

AUSTIN: You can't just drop the whole thing, Lee!

[LEE *turns, pushes* AUSTIN *in the chest, knocking him backwards into the alcove.* MOM *watches numbly,* LEE *returns to collecting the plates, silverware, etc.*]

MOM: You boys shouldn't fight in the house. Go outside and fight.

LEE: I'm not fightin'. I'm leavin'.

MOM: There's been enough damage done already.

LEE: [*His back to* AUSTIN *and* MOM, *stacking dishes on counter*] I'm clearin' outa' here once and for all. All this town does is drive a man insane. Look what it's done to Austin there. I'm not lettin' that happen to me. Sell myself down the river. No sir. I'd rather be a hundred miles from nowhere than let that happen to me.

[*During this,* AUSTIN *has picked up the ripped-out phone from the floor and wrapped the cord tightly around both his hands. He lunges at* LEE *whose back is still to him, wraps the cord around* LEE'*s neck, plants a foot in* LEE'*s back and pulls back on the cord, tightening it.* LEE *chokes desperately, can't speak and can't reach* AUSTIN *with his arms.* AUSTIN *keeps applying pressure on* LEE'*s back with his foot, bending him into the sink.* MOM *watches*.]

AUSTIN: [*Tightening cord*] You're not goin' anywhere! You're not takin' anything with you. You're not takin' my car! You're not takin' the dishes! You're not takin' anything! You're stayin' right here!

▷ **1** *keep in touch:* not to lose contact with sb. • *get out of touch:* lose contact with sb. **6** *numb* [nʌm]: unable to think, feel or react in the normal way **14** *sell sb. down the river* (infml): betray sb., treat sb. in an unfair way **20** *choke:* gasp or struggle for air

MOM: You'll have to stop fighting in the house. There's plenty of room outside to fight. You've got the whole outdoors to fight in.

[LEE *tries to tear himself away. He crashes across the stage like an enraged bull, dragging* AUSTIN *with him. He snorts and bellows but* AUSTIN *hangs on and manages to keep clear of* LEE'*s attempts to grab him. They crash into the table, to the floor.* LEE *is face down thrashing wildly and choking,* AUSTIN *pulls cord tighter, stands with one foot planted on* LEE'*s back and the cord stretched taut.*]

AUSTIN: [*Holding cord*] Gimme back my keys, Lee! Take the keys out! Take 'em out!

[LEE *desperately tries to dig in his pockets, searching for the car keys.* MOM *moves closer.*]

MOM: [*Calmly to* AUSTIN] You're not killing him are you?

AUSTIN: I don't know. I don't know if I'm killing him. I'm stopping him. That's all. I'm just stopping him.

[LEE *thrashes but* AUSTIN *is relentless.*]

MOM: You oughta' let him breathe a little bit.

AUSTIN: Throw the keys out, Lee!

[LEE *finally gets keys out and throws them on floor but out of* AUSTIN'*s reach.* AUSTIN *keeps pressure on cord, pulling* LEE'*s neck back.* LEE *gets one hand to the cord but can't relieve the pressure.*]

Reach me those keys would ya', Mom?

MOM: [*Not moving*] Why are you doing this to him?

AUSTIN: Reach me the keys!

MOM: Not until you stop choking him.

AUSTIN: I can't stop choking him! He'll kill me if I stop choking him!

▷ **4** *snort:* schnauben • *bellow:* make a noise like a bull **7** *thrash* (v): make violent movements **8** *taut* [tɑːt]: stiff; very tight **16** *relentless:* not willing to give in or stop **22** *reach me sth.:* reach out and hand me sth.

MOM: He won't kill you. He's your brother.

AUSTIN: Just get me the keys would ya'!

[*Pause.* MOM *picks keys off floor, hands them to* AUSTIN.]

[*To* MOM] Thanks.

MOM: Will you let him go now?

AUSTIN: I don't know. He's not gonna' let me get outa' here.

MOM: Well you can't kill him.

AUSTIN: I can kill him! I can easily kill him. Right now. Right here. All I gotta' do is just tighten up. See?

[AUSTIN *tightens cord,* LEE *thrashes wildly,* AUSTIN *releases pressure a little, maintaining control.*]

Ya' see that?

MOM: That's a savage thing to do.

AUSTIN: Yeah well don't tell me I can't kill him, because I can. I can just twist. I can keep twisting.

[AUSTIN *twists the cord tighter,* LEE *weakens, his breathing changes to a short rasp.*]

MOM: Austin!

[AUSTIN *relieves pressure,* LEE *breathes easier but* AUSTIN *keeps him under control.*]

AUSTIN: [*Eyes on* LEE, *holding cord*] I'm goin' to the desert. There's nothing stopping me. I'm going by myself to the desert.

MOM: [*Moving toward her luggage*] Well, I'm going to go check into a motel. I can't stand this anymore.

▷ **13** *savage:* brutal; cruel **17** *rasp* (n): (here) harsh sound made by sb. trying hard to breathe

AUSTIN: Don't go yet!

[MOM *pauses.*]

MOM: I can't stay here. This is worse than being homeless.

AUSTIN: I'll get everything fixed up for you, Mom. I promise. Just stay for a while.

MOM: [*Picking up luggage*] You're going to the desert.

AUSTIN: Just wait!

[LEE *thrashes,* AUSTIN *subdues him,* MOM *watches, holding luggage. Pause*]

MOM: It was the worst feeling being up there. In Alaska. Staring out a window. I never felt so desperate before. That's why when I saw that article on Picasso I thought –

AUSTIN: Stay here, Mom. This is where you live –

[MOM *looks around the stage.*]

MOM: I don't recognize it at all.

[MOM *exits with luggage,* AUSTIN *makes a move toward her but* LEE *starts to struggle and* AUSTIN *subdues him again with cord. Pause*]

AUSTIN: [*Holding cord*] Lee? I'll make ya' a deal. You let me get outa' here. Just let me get to my car. All right, Lee? Gimme a little headstart and I'll turn you loose. Just gimme a little headstart. All right?

[LEE *makes no response,* AUSTIN *slowly releases tension on cord, still nothing from* LEE.]

Lee?

▷ **8** *subdue sb.:* get sb. under your control **11** *desperate:* hopeless, depressed **20** *headstart:* Vorsprung

[LEE *is motionless,* AUSTIN *very slowly begins to stand, still keeping a tenuous hold on the cord and his eyes riveted to* LEE *for any sign of movement.* AUSTIN *slowly drops the cord and stands, he stares down at* LEE *who appears to be dead.*]

AUSTIN: [*Whispers*] Lee?

[*Pause.* AUSTIN *considers, looks toward exit, back to* LEE, *then makes a small movement as if to leave. Instantly* LEE *is on his feet and moves toward exit, blocking* AUSTIN*'s escape. They square off to each other, keeping a distance between them. Pause. A single coyote heard in distance, lights fade softly into moonlight, the figures of the brothers now appear to be caught in a vast desert-like landscape. They are very still but watchful for the next move. Lights go slowly to black as the after-image of the brothers pulses in the dark, coyote fades.*]

▷ **2** *tenuous:* (here) weak but careful • *riveted to:* fixed to **8** *square off* (infml): stand in a position that shows you are prepared to fight **13** *after-image:* impression of a sensation retained by the eyes after the real image has disappeared

ADDITIONAL TEXTS

I. The Archetypal Fraternal Struggle

1

Cain and Abel

Abel, the second son of Adam and Eve, was a shepherd and his brother Cain a farmer. They both made an offering to God from the fruits of their labor. Because of Abel's faith his sacrifice was judged greater than Cain's, whose sacrifice was rejected by God. It is interesting to note that the first time brothers are mentioned in the Bible, they fight.

The Lord received Abel and his gift with favour; but Cain and his gift he did not receive.

Cain was very angry and his face fell. Then the Lord said to Cain, "why are you so angry and cast down?

If you do well, you hold your head up; if not, sin is a demon crouching at the door. It shall be eager for you, but you must master it."

Cain said to his brother Abel, "Let us go into the open country." While they were there, Cain attacked his brother Abel and murdered him.

Then the Lord said to Cain, "Where is you brother Abel?" Cain answered, "I do not know. Am I my brother's keeper?"

The Lord said, "What have you done? Hark! Your brother's blood that has been shed is crying out to me from the ground.

Now you are accursed, and banished from the ground which has opened its mouth wide to receive your brother's blood which you have shed;

When you till the ground, it will no longer yield you its wealth: You shall be a vagrant and a wanderer on earth."

Cain said to the Lord, "My punishment is heavier than I can bear;

▷ **6** *crouch:* hocken, kauern **13** *hark* (old use): listen **15** *accursed:* verflucht **18** *till the ground:* den Boden bestellen • *yield sth.:* produce sth., provide sth.

Thou hast driven me today from the ground, and I must hide myself from thy presence. I shall be a vagrant and a wanderer on earth, and anyone who meets me can kill me."

The Lord answered him, "No: if anyone kills Cain, Cain shall be avenged sevenfold." So the Lord put a mark on Cain, in order that anyone meeting him should not kill him.

Then Cain went out from the Lord's presence and settled in the land of Nod to the east of Eden.

(From: *Genesis* 4, 4–16, *The New English Bible*, Oxford University Press, Cambridge University Press, 1970)

▷ **21** *thou* (old use): you **22** *vagrant* ['veɪgrənt]: homeless person **28** *east of Eden:* the garden of Eden is heaven on earth (cf. also the title of Steinbeck's novel, p. 101)

2

Jacob and Esau

Isaac and Rebecca had twins, Jacob and Esau. As the latter was born first he was regarded as the heir to his father. However, despite this tradition the Lord had told Rebecca that her older son would serve the younger son. The two brothers are often seen as personifying the struggle between the hunter civilization (Esau is the hairy hunter) and the settler civilization (Jacob is the smooth man who founded the nation of Israel).

Isaac appealed to the Lord on behalf of his wife because she was barren; the Lord yielded to his entreaty, and Rebecca conceived.

The children pressed hard on each other in her womb, and she said, 'If this is how it is with me, what does it mean?' So she went to seek guidance of the Lord.

The Lord said to her: 'Two nations in your womb, two peoples, going their own ways from birth! One shall be stronger than the other; the older shall be servant to the younger.'

When her time had come, there were indeed twins in her womb.

The first came out red, hairy all over like a hair-cloak, and they named him Esau.

Immediately afterwards his brother was born with his hand grasping Esau's heel, and they called him Jacob. Isaac was sixty years old when they were born.

The boys grew up; and Esau became skilful in hunting, a man of the open plains, but Jacob led a settled life and stayed among the tents.

Isaac favoured Esau because he kept him supplied with venison, but Rebecca favoured Jacob.

▷ **2** *barren:* infertile, childless • *yield to sth.:* agree to sth., grant sth. • *entreaty:* request • *conceive:* become pregnant **3** *press hard on:* (here) fight, struggle • *womb* [wu:m]: (Mutter)Leib **10** *cloak:* Mantel **18** *venison:* meat from a deer

With Rebecca's help, Jacob tricks his blind father, Isaac, into giving him the fatherly blessing that is supposed to go to the oldest son.

Esau bore a grudge against Jacob because of the blessing which his father had given him, and he said to himself, "The time of mourning for my father will soon be here; then I will kill my brother Jacob."

When Rebecca was told what her eldest son Esau was saying, she called her younger son Jacob, and she said to him, "Esau your brother is threatening to kill you.

Now, my son, listen to me. Slip away at once to my brother Laban in Harran.

Stay with him for a while until your brother's anger cools.

When it has subsided and he forgets what you have done to him, I will send and fetch you back. Why should I lose you both in one day?"

(From: Genesis, *The New English Bible*, Oxford University Press, Cambridge University Press, 1970)

▷ **20** *bear a grudge against sb.:* jdm. grollen **21** *mourn:* feel extreme sadness at the death of sb. **27** *Harran:* ancient town where Abraham's family settled **29** *subside:* become less

3

Cal and Aron

The following text is an excerpt from the last chapter of John Steinbeck's novel *East of Eden* (1952) a long family saga covering the period from the American Civil War to the First World War. Using the theme of Cain and Abel, the novel examines humanity's struggle between good and evil.

Adam Trask, a farmer, marries Cathy Ames, an ex-prostitute who is depicted as the personification of evil. After the birth of her twins, Calec (Cal) and Aron, she leaves her husband and children. Aron is generous, easy-going and loving, and is his father's favourite, while Caleb is wild and lacks self-control; he sets in motion the sequence of events leading to a final tragedy. He tells his brother about their mother; Aron then joins the army and is sent to fight in Europe in the First World War.

All the lights were on in the Trask house. The door stood partly open, and the house was cold. In the sitting room Lee was shriveled up like a leaf in the chair beside the lamp. Adam's door was open and the sound of voices came from his room.

When Cal came in he asked, "What's going on?"

Lee looked at him and swung his head toward the table where the open telegram lay. "Your brother is dead," he said. "Your father has had a stroke."

[...] Cal moved away and walked toward his father's room.

Adam's head was propped up on pillows. His face was calm, the skin pale; his mouth was straight, neither smiling nor disapproving. His eyes were open, and they had great depth and clarity, as though one could see deep into them and as though they could see deep into their surroundings. And the eyes were calm, aware but not interested. They turned slowly toward Cal as he entered the room, found his chest, and then rose to his face and stayed there.

▷ *East of Eden:* cf. Genesis 4:16 (p. 98, l. 28) **2** *Lee:* the Trask family's Chinese cook • *shriveled up:* dried up **8** *stroke* (n): Schlaganfall **10** *prop sth. up:* support sth. by putting things (here: pillows) under it **16** *chest:* breast

Cal sat down in the straight chair beside the bed. He said, "I'm sorry, Father."

The eyes blinked slowly the way a frog blinks.

"Can you hear me, Father? Can you understand me?" The eyes did not change or move. "I did it," Cal cried. "I'm responsible for Aron's death and for your sickness. I took him to Kate's. I showed him his mother. That's why he went away. I don't want to do bad things – but I do them."

He put his head down on the side of the bed to escape the terrible eyes, and he could still see them. He knew they would be with him, a part of him, all of his life.

The doorbell rang. In a moment Lee came to the bedroom. [...]

Lee asked softly, "Did he speak to you?"

Cal shook his head back and forth as though he couldn't stop.

"It's going to be dreadful. But the doctor is right. You can stand anything. We're wonderful animals that way."

"I'm not." Cal's voice was flat and dull. "I can't stand it. No, I can't stand it. I won't be able to. I'll have to – I'll have to –"

Lee gripped his wrist fiercely. "Why, you mouse – you nasty cur. With goodness all around you – don't you dare suggest a thing like that! Why is your sorrow more refined than my sorrow?"

"It's not sorrow. I told him what I did. I killed my brother. I'm a murderer. He knows it."

"Did he say it? Tell the truth – did he say it?"

"He didn't have to. It was in his eyes. He said it with his eyes.. There's nowhere I can go to get away – there's no place."

Lee sighed and released his wrist. "Cal" – he spoke patiently – "listen to me. Adam's brain centers are affected. Anything you see in his eyes may be pressure on that part of his brain which governs his seeing. Don't you remember? – he couldn't read. That wasn't his eyes – that was pressure. You don't know he accused you. You don't know that."

"He accused me. I know it. He said I'm a murderer."

▷ **19** *blink:* shut and open your eyes quickly **22** *Kate's:* brothel owned by Cathy, the mother of the twins **35** *nasty:* unpleasant • *cur:* Köter **43** *sigh:* (auf)seufzen

"Then he will forgive you. I promise." […]

[Cal] walked slowly down the walk and turned toward home, and he hadn't gone a block before Abra caught up with him. […]

Cal said, "Abra, I've killed my brother and my father is paralysed because of me."

She took his arm and clung to it with both hands.

Cal said, "Didn't you hear me?"

"I heard you."

"Abra, my mother was a whore."

"I know. You told me. My father is a thief."

"I've got her blood, Abra. Don't you understand?"

"I've got his," she said.

They walked along in silence while he tried to rebalance himself. […]

When they trooped into the bedroom Adam was propped high on his pillows […].

Lee and Cal and Abra stood at the foot of the bed, and Adam's eyes moved slowly from one face to the other, and his lips moved just a little in greeting.

[…] Lee's voice cut in, "I don't know how long you will live, Adam. Maybe a long time. Maybe an hour. But your son will live. He will marry and his children will be the only remnant left of you.' Lee wiped his eyes with his fingers.

"He did a thing in anger, Adam, because he thought you had rejected him. The result of his anger is that his brother and your son is dead."

Cal said, "Lee – you can't."

"I have to," said Lee. "If it kills him I have to. I have the choice," and he smiled sadly and quoted, " 'If there's a blame, it's my blame.' " Lee's shoulders straightened. He said sharply. 'Your son is marked

▷ **52** *Abra:* a young woman who likes Aron, but who Cal tries to win over • *catch up with sb.:* reach sb. who is walking ahead **58** *whore:* prostitute **62** *rebalance yourself:* steady yourself again; give yourself (mental) balance **71** *remnant:* remaining thing

with guilt out of himself – out of himself – almost more than he can bear. Don't crush him with rejection. Don't crush him, Adam."

Lee's breath whistled in his throat. "Adam, give him your blessing. Don't leave him alone with his guilt." [...]

Adam looked up with sick weariness. His lips parted and failed and tried again. Then his lungs filled. He expelled the air and his lips combed the rushing sigh. His whispered word seemed to hang in the air:

"*Timshel*!"

His eyes closed and he slept.

(From: John Steinbeck, *East of Eden*. Copyright © 1952 by John Steinbeck; copyright © renewed by Elaine Steinbeck, Thom Steinbeck, and John Steinbeck IV, 1980. Reprinted wth the permission of McIntosh and Otis, inc.

▷ **81** *crush sb.:* destroy sb. **84** *part:* open **85** *expel sth.:* let sth. out **88** *timshel* (Hebrew): You may (rule over sin), i.e. you can choose between good and evil

II. The American Dream – Then and Now

4

The American Dream

This excerpt is from James Truslow Adams's *The Epic of America* (1931). It was Adams (1878–1949) who coined the term 'the American dream'. *The Epic of America* is a popular history book that also offers an analysis of the American character, which Adams defines as the 'dream for a better, richer, and happier life for all our citizens of every rank.'

'The American Dream' is that dream of a land in which life should be better and richer and fuller for everyone, with opportunity for each according to ability or achievement. It is a difficult dream for the European upper classes to interpret adequately, and too many of us ourselves have grown weary and mistrustful of it. It is not a dream of motor cars and high wages merely, but a dream of social order in which each man and each woman shall be able to attain to the fullest stature of which they are innately capable, and be recognized by others for what they are, regardless of the fortuitous circumstances of birth or position. […] [This] dream that has lured tens of millions of all nations to our shores in the past century has not been a dream of merely plenty, though that has doubtless counted heavily. It has been much more than that. It has been a dream of being able to grow to fullest development as man and woman, unhampered by the barriers which had slowly been erected in older civilizations, unrepressed by social orders which had developed for the benefit of classes rather than for the simple human being of any and every class. And that dream has been realized more fully in actual life here than anywhere else […]

(From: James Truslow Adams, *The Epic of America*, 1931)

▷ **5** *weary:* tired • *mistrustful:* suspicious; sceptical **7** *attain sth.:* achieve sth. • *stature* ['stætʃə]: status, position **8** *innate:* inborn **9** *fortuitous* [fɔːr'tuːətəs]: happening by chance **10** *lure sb.:* attract sb. **14** *unhampered:* not hindered or held back **15** *erect sth.:* establish sth., create sth.

5

The Ideal of Human Brotherhood

The following text is taken from Martin Luther King's most famous speech, which was delivered on the steps at the Lincoln Memorial in Washington D.C. during the "March on Washington", the famous civil rights demonstration on August 28, 1963.

I have a dream that one day this nation will rise up and live out the true meaning of its creed: "We hold these truths to be self-evident: that all men are created equal."

I have a dream that one day on the red hills of Georgia the sons of former slaves and the sons of former slave-owners will be able to sit down together at a table of brotherhood.

I have a dream that one day even the state of Mississippi, a desert state, sweltering with the heat of injustice and oppression, will be transformed into an oasis of freedom and justice.

I have a dream that my four little children will one day live in a nation where they will not be judged by the color of their skin but by the content of their character.

I have a dream that one day the state of Alabama, whose governor's lips are presently dripping with the words of interposition and nullification, will be transformed into a situation where little black boys and black girls will be able to join hands with little white boys and white girls as sisters and brothers.

I have a dream that one day every valley shall be exalted, every hill and mountain shall be made low, the rough places will be made plain, and the crooked places will be made straight, and the glory of the Lord shall be revealed, and all flesh shall see it together. This is our hope. This is the faith with which I return to the South.

▷ **2** *creed:* belief **8** *sweltering:* suffering from heat **12** *content of their character:* elements that form their personalities **14–15** *interposition and nullification:* principles which give each state of the USA the right to reject any federal law it regards as a violation of the sovereign right of the state **18** *exalt sth.:* raise sth. in power and dignity **20** *crooked:* not straight

With this faith we will be able to hew out of the mountain of despair a stone of hope. With this faith we will be able to transform the jangling discords of our nation into a beautiful symphony of brotherhood. With this faith we will be able to work together, to pray together, to struggle together, to go to jail together, to stand up for freedom together, knowing that we will be free one day.

▷ **23** *hew:* cut, shape **25** *jangling:* unpleasant • *discords:* disharmony

6

Letter to a Vietnamese Cousin: Should You Come to America?

The following letter was written by Andrew Lam and published by NCM (New California Media) in 2003. Andrew Lam was born in Vietnam. In 1975 when he was 11 years old he went to the USA as a refugee. He studied biochemistry at UC Berkeley and then creative writing at San Francisco State University. Plagued with a deep longing to make use of his Vietnamese memories, he decided to start a career as a journalist writing for the Pacific News Service. He is also a short story writer. His first book to be published is *Perfume Dreams: Reflections on the Vietnamese Diaspora* (2005).

Dear Cousin D.,

What is it like to be an immigrant in America these days? Is it still worth coming, and is the dream still possible?

Your questions, I must admit, gave me pause. Who, after all, would have thought to ask them a few years back from Vietnam? Didn't the American Dream, or rather, the dreaming of coming to America, cause the movement of millions in our homeland, and stir the soul of many millions more?

It breaks my heart then to hear that you might not come. It is to me the worst news yet about my adopted country.

Yet it's undeniable. The nation of immigrants is turning its back on immigrants once more. There is a fundamental shift here, and I fear it is for the worst. Since that terrible day of Sept. 11 of last year, that ominous cloud from the debris of those fallen twin towers seems to have hovered permanently over our once blue and gracious sky.

▷ *New California Media*: association of more than 400 ethnic media organizations in California **4** *give pause to sb.*: make sb. think seriously **7** *stir sb.*: move sb.'s feelings **12** *shift:* change **13** *Sept. 11:* the attacks on the World Trade Center by terrorists in 2001 **14** *debris* [də'bri:]: Trümmer

The condition, compared to just a few years ago, is no longer what you would call optimal. The borders are much harder to cross for many, and the threat of terrorism has shaken our sense of safety to the core. The immigrant's hold on American soil, as a direct result, has become increasingly tenuous, if not outright threatened.

Cousin, have you heard the metaphor of the canary bird in the mine? When it stops singing, it means the oxygen is going out of the place, a warning to all.

In America, and in the context of a free and open society, often the immigrant is that canary. In economic down times he is often the first to be blamed. And in the U.S. war against terrorism, he is fast becoming the scapegoat.

In the name of protection and security, immigrants' rights are being eroded as I write. The new U.S.A.-Patriot Act has devastating results as arrests can be made without warrants, and suspects can be held without charges for prolonged periods. Unchecked surveillance and secret detentions by the U.S. government of Arabs and Muslims in America is growing. I know many Muslims are now afraid to pray at their own mosque for fear of FBI surveillance. I've seen feeble old South Asian women whose hands trembled at the airport when they give their green cards to immigration officers, fearing sudden arrest and deportation. These days an immigrant can lose his job because he is not yet a U.S. citizen, and if he speaks his opinion, he can very well be fired.

Worse, what once were minor infractions can now turn into a major disaster. For instance, failing to report to the INS your change of address when you move could mean being deported back to a country from which you fled – a cruel and unusual punishment if you

▷ **18–19** *to the core:* fundamentally **20** *tenuous:* delicate, fragile • *outright:* completely **22** *oxygen:* Sauerstoff **27** *scapegoat:* Sündenbock **29** *erode sth.:* gradually destroy sth. or make it weaker **30** *warrant:* official, written permission for the police to arrest sb. **31** *charge:* formal accusation that sb. has committed a crime **32** *detention:* imprisonment of sb. without being charged with a crime **34** *mosque* [mɑːsk]: Moschee **40** *infraction:* act of doing sth. that breaks the law but is not criminal **41** *INS:* Immigration and Naturalization Service

happen to be an Iranian or Syrian refugee fleeing from a vindictive regime.

Cousin, I do not know how effective homeland security is, but I know that it has already brought much insecurity to large segments of society. Within our own community, far from the turmoil and passion of the Middle East and South Asia, I nevertheless also hear a prudent whisper, and it's the kind that sends a chill down my back: They know. Cousin C. was looking at my library card the other day, and he said: 'They know.'

Know what, I asked.

'With the new technology, the government can tell what books you are checking out of the library, what you buy,' he said. 'Be careful. They know.'

This, mind you, is the same man who was inspired during the high-tech boom, by the new information revolution that was changing the world for the better, and giving equal footing to so many. Today, laid-off from a software engineering job, he sees the technology he admired so much has turned into war machines for an empire. It turns into drones and satellites to seek out enemies abroad, and at home. It turns into an ominous electronic eye – the all-seeing eye of homeland security that never blinks – that can monitor and spy on immigrants and perhaps, soon, everyone else living in America.

A new program called Total Information Awareness might be installed here, especially if there is another terrorist attack. It is being developed by a Pentagon division, one that amazingly gave birth to the Internet. [...] I fear that the program will, in the process, turn this country into a kind of police state that would make communist Vietnam look like Club Med. Electronic internment camp is a turn of phrase I hear whispered among many Arab Americans.

You don't have to be behind barbed wire like the Japanese Americans during World War II anymore, they say, but the effect is essentially the same.

▷ **44** *vindictive:* revengeful **48** *turmoil:* confusion **49** *prudent:* wise **59** *footing* (n): status or relationship between two things **62** *drone:* unmanned remote piloted aircraft **64** *blink:* zwinkern • *monitor sth.:* observe and check on sth. **71** *Club Med:* company that runs its own holiday resorts **73** *barbed wire:* Stacheldraht

They know. And so it is true, cousin, in America, the sky has eyes, and walls have ears. And the ground, too, can feel the tremor of your every footstep. Ruben Martinez, a Mexican-American friend and writer, told me he once walked a few feet back and forth across the border of Mexico and Texas in the middle of nowhere, and a few minutes later border patrol cars surrounded him. 'How did you know that I was here?' he asked. 'We have sensors that feel vibration along the border,' said the border patrol man, 'and you sir, have just violated a law.'

A young Chinese American student at UC Berkeley who, in the discussion of a video game, mentioned the word 'bomb' several times on the phone, and within the next hour three police officers knocked at her dormitory door. She and her roommate were interrogated thoroughly. She still doesn't know how they know, but, apparently, they know.

Alas, the general public is little aware of what is going on in the lives of those on the sweeping reach of government dragnets. In their yearning for safety and protection, they already supported the new law that imprisons anyone without due process, and punishes dissent. Perhaps they don't want to know. But when a society hides behind the apparatus of draconian policy, one that has no check and balance, the only logical outcome is injustice and cruelty.

Over the years I find it beneficial to look at this country through two different lenses: America versus the United States. The United States is a sovereign country with permanent interests that is currently waging a war on terrorism.

And it will trample upon innocents in its path, be it at home or abroad, if need be, in order to win it. In the process, the newcomer to this country, one without a voice and resources, often becomes collateral damage.

▷ **77** *tremor:* (here) vibration **83** *violate sth.:* break or disobey sth. **85** *UC Berkeley:* University of California at Berkeley **88** *dormitory:* university building in which students live **92** *dragnet:* Fangnetz **93** *yearning:* longing **94** *due process:* the proper course of legal action **95** *dissent:* disagreement, opposition **96** *draconian:* harsh, severe **98** *beneficial:* helpful, advantageous **104** *resources:* wealth, natural supply of raw goods **105** *collateral:* additional; that is affected by accident

America, on the other hand, is everything you and I ever dreamed of – transparency, freedom, democracy, opportunity, due process, fair play and a premise of progress. America is where you work hard and earn respect, find a job and raise your kids in peace, and the government does not raid your home to take you away in the middle of the night because of the way you look, or the religion you practice. America tolerates differences, understands diversity and does not assume you are guilty before proven innocent.

The two versions exist in a kind of complex dance. In good times, America leads and in bad, America is forgotten and the United States dances alone. These days, I fear that to be a patriotic immigrant is to love the ideals of America despite what the United States is doing in the name of patriotism and security.

While I understand the logic of permanent interest, if America is destroyed in the process, then what is the use? And as far as I am concerned the only good patriotism is a civilized one. Blind patriotism always leads to a bloody end and unchecked government that functions behind the veil of secrecy and should never be tolerated. To be patriotic is to dare ask questions. Must rights be abused in the name of security? What is it that is protected when freedom is given up wholesale?

Dear cousin, I hope I haven't completely frightened you, but the situation requires honesty. To reach the American shore these days is a much more difficult undertaking, with fewer ready-made promises at the horizon. People are still coming, albeit at the threat of deportation and false arrests. They come, in spite of everything, because their willpower is made of fire and steel.

I still want you to make this difficult journey, but you must be prepared for the challenges ahead. And I'll let you in on a secret about this American Dream you spoke so fondly of: It is you who renews it. Without you, who dreams the American dream, the country is in danger of becoming old. Without your energy, we would weaken.

▷ **108** *premise:* (here) belief that sth. is true **110** *raid sth.:* search sth. **113** *assume:* believe, suppose **123** *veil:* Schleier **126** *wholesale:* totally **130** *albeit* [ɑːlˈbiːɪt] (fml): although **134** *let sb. in on a secret* (infml): share a secret with sb.

Even if we don't know it yet, we all desperately need to be reborn through your eyes.

So, is the American Dream still alive?

No, cousin, not really. Not without you at the table, not without you prospering, not without you.

(From: Andrew Lam, *New California Media*, Jan 6, 2003; printed by kind permission of the author)

▷ **142** *prosper:* do well, be successful

III. Aspects of the West

7

The Mojave Desert

In his travel book *Travels with Charley: In Search of America* (1962), John Steinbeck's last important full-length work before his death six years later, the author describes his journey through the USA with his dog Charley. "In the Desert" is the title of a chapter from this book and relates his experiences in the Mojave Desert.

The Mojave is a big desert and a frightening one. It's as though nature tested a man for endurance and constancy to prove whether he was good enough to get to California. The shimmering dry heat made visions of water on the flat plain. And even when you drive at high speed, the hills that mark the boundaries recede before you. Charley, always a dog for water, panted asthmatically, jarring his whole body with the effort, and a good eight inches of his tongue hung out flat as a leaf and dripping. I pulled off the road into a small gully to give him water from my thirty-gallon tank. But before I let him drink I poured water all over him and on my hair and shoulder and shirt. The air is so dry that evaporation makes you feel suddenly cold.

I opened a can of beer from my refrigerator and sat well inside the shade of Rocinante, looking out at the sun-pounded plain, dotted here and there with clumps of sagebrush.

About fifty yards away two coyotes stood watching me, their tawny coats blending with the sand and sun. I knew that with any quick or

▷ **3** *shimmer:* shine with a soft light that seems to move **5** *recede:* move back **6** *pant:* breathe quickly and loudly with an open mouth • *jar sth.:* make sth. tremble **8** *gully:* deep ditch formed by rain water **9** *gallon:* (in the USA) ca. 3.8 litres **11** *evaporation:* Verdunstung **13** *Rocinante* [rɔːsɪ'nænti]: name of Steinbeck's vehicle (taken from the name of Don Quixote's horse) • *sun-pounded:* beaten down by the sun • *dotted:* covered **14** *clump:* (here) group • *sagebrush:* North American shrub common in the dry western plains (= Beifuß) **15** *tawny:* yellowish brown **16** *blend with sth.:* become one with sth., mix with sth.

suspicious movement of mine they could drift into invisibility. With the most casual slowness I reached down my new rifle from its sling over my bed – the.222 with its bitter little high-speed, long-range stings. Very slowly I brought the rifle up. Perhaps in the shade of my house I was half hidden by the blinding light outside. The little rifle has a beautiful telescope sight with a wide field. The coyotes had not moved.

I got both of them in the field of my telescope, and the glass brought them very close. Their tongues lolled out so that they seemed to smile mockingly. They were favored animals, not starved, but well furred, the golden hair tempered with black guard hairs. Their little lemon-yellow eyes were plainly visible in the glass. I moved the cross hairs to the breast of the right-hand animal, and pushed the safety. My elbows on the table steadied the gun. The cross hairs lay unmoving on the brisket. And then the coyote sat down like a dog and its right rear paw came up to scratch the right shoulder.

My finger was reluctant to touch the trigger. I must be getting very old and my ancient conditioning worn thin. Coyotes are vermin. They steal chickens. They thin the ranks of quail and all other game birds. They must be killed. They are the enemy. My first shot would drop the sitting beast, and the other would whirl to fade away. I might very well pull him down with a running shot because I am a good rifleman.

And I did not fire. My training said, "Shoot!" and my age replied, "There isn't a chicken within thirty miles, and if there are any they aren't my chickens. And this waterless place is not quail country. No,

▷ **18** *casual:* lässig **19** *the .222:* gun well known for its accuracy and efficiency **20** *sting:* shot **25** *lol out:* hang out loosely **26** *favored:* (here) looking healthy **27** *furred:* covered with fur • *tempered with sth.:* mixed with sth., slightly altered by sth. • *guard hairs:* long straight hair that grows over the fur of an animal **28–29** *cross hairs:* Fadenkreuz **29** *push the safety:* entsichern **31** *brisket:* the breast of an animal **32** *rear paw:* back foot of an animal that has claws or nails **33** *reluctant:* unwilling, hesitant • *trigger:* (Gewehr)Abzug **34** *conditioning:* upbringing that determines how one behaves • *vermin:* animals and birds that are harmful to crops and farm animals (e.g. rats, rabbits, etc.) **35** *thin the ranks of sth.:* lessen the number of sth. • *quail:* Wachtel **37** *fade away:* (here) flee, disappear **38** *running shot:* shot aimed at a running animal

these boys are keeping their figures with kangaroo rats and jackrabbits, and that's vermin eat vermin. Why should I interfere?" [...]

I have driven through the Southwest many times, and even more often have flown over it – a great and mysterious wasteland, a sun-punished place. It is a mystery, something concealed and waiting. It seems deserted, free of parasitic man, but this is not entirely so. Follow the double line of wheel tracks through sand and rock and you will find a habitation somewhere huddled in a protected place, with a few trees pointing their roots at under-earth water, a patch of starveling corn and squash, and strips of jerky hanging on a string. There is a breed of desert men, not hiding exactly but gone to sanctuary from the sins of confusion.

At night in this waterless air the stars come down just out of reach of your fingers. In such a place lived the hermits of the early church piercing to infinity with unlittered minds. The great concepts of oneness and of majestic order seem always to be born in the desert. The quiet counting of the stars, and observation of their movements, came first from desert places. I have known desert men who chose their places with quiet and slow passion, rejecting the nervousness of a watered world. These men have not changed with the exploding times except to die and be replaced by others like them.

And always there are mysteries in the desert, stories told and retold of secret places in the desert mountains where surviving clans from an older era wait to re-emerge. Usually these groups guard treasures hidden from the waves of conquest, the golden artifacts of an archaic Montezuma, or a mime so rich that its discovery would change the world. If a stranger discovers their existence, he is killed or so ab-

▷ **43** *keep your figure:* remain healthy-looking • *kangaroo rat:* small animal found in the dry and desert regions of North America **43–44** *jackrabbit:* type of North American hare **47** *concealed:* hidden **50** *huddled:* zusamengekauert **52** *starveling* ['stɑːvlɪŋ]: miserable • *squash* (AE): Kürbis • *jerky* (AE): meat that is cut in long strips and then dried in the sun **53** *breed:* type **53–54** *sanctuary:* (here) lonely place of refuge **56** *hermit:* Eremit(in) **57** *unlittered:* (here) clear **58** *oneness:* the feeling of being in harmony with nature and the universe **66** *re-emerge:* reappear, turn up again **67** *artifact:* product of human art **68** *Montezuma:* the last Aztec emperor of Mexico, who was captured by the Spanish

sorbed that he is never seen again. These stories have an inevitable pattern untroubled by the question, If none return, how is it known what is there? Oh, it's there all right, but if you find it you will never be found.

And there is another monolithic tale which never changes. Two prospectors in partnership discover a mine of preternatural richness – of gold or diamonds or rubies. They load themselves with samples, as much as they can carry, and they mark the place in their minds by landmarks all around. Then, on the way out to the other world, one dies of thirst and exhaustion, but the other crawls on, discarding most of the treasure he has grown too weak to carry. He comes at last to a settlement, or perhaps is found by other prospecting men. They examine his samples with great excitement. Sometimes in the story the survivor dies after leaving directions with his rescuers, or again he is nursed back to strength. Then a well-equipped party sets out to find the treasure, and it can never be found again. That is the invariable end of the story – it is never found again. I have heard this story many times, and it never changes. There is nourishment in the desert for myth, but myth must somewhere have its roots in reality.

(From: John Steinbeck, *Travels with Charley: In Search of America.* Copyright © The Curtis Publishing Co., Inc., 1961, 1962; Copyright © 1962 by John Steinbeck; Copyright © renewed by Elaine Steinbeck, Thom Steinbeck, and John Steinbeck IV 1989, 1990. Reprinted with the permission of McIntosh and Otis, Inc.)

▷ **69–70** *be absorbed:* become part of sth. **74** *monolithic:* monumental **75** *prospector:* person searching for gold • *preternatural:* extraordinary, unusual **79** *crawl:* move very slowly on your hands and knees • *discard sth.:* throw sth. away, get rid of sth. **81** *prospecting:* searching for gold

8

Cowboys

The well-known British novelist, playwright, and essayist J.B. Priestley (1894–1984) also wrote several non-fictional works. The following text is an excerpt from *Midnight on the Desert* (the first volume of his autobiography), a book that deals with the experiences he made during the winter of 1935–36 when he spent several months in Arizona anonymously working on Hollywood screenplays.

[A cowboy's] life may be infinitely narrower than that of an artist or a scientist, but can it be said to be any narrower than the existence of all those pale-faced millions who go day after day to factories, warehouses, offices and shops, the victims of all the cunningly deployed forces of publicity and salesmanship, of rubber-stamp opinions and artificially stimulated wants? He is at peace with himself because his work allows free play to the strongest instinct of man. Unlike so many other men, he has not to pretend to be a short-sighted, deaf cripple all day to earn his living, and then to try and catch up with himself as a vital human being during the short hours of leisure allotted to him. His work is not without danger, and he is sustained by a sense of this, knowing that he has a certain fundamental dignity. This is true of other kinds of men, such as the miner and the sailor, men who are shabbily treated by the community they serve, but are often inwardly sustained by their sense of being engaged in an heroic calling. This is joined in the cowboy to an outward picturesqueness and a magnificent stage setting. There is still a good book to be written about the legend of the heroic West and the cowboy. The author would have to be a social philosopher as well as an historian. The legend has not been with us long. That West had a

▷ **5** *deploy sth.:* put sth. into a position to achieve a particular result • *rubber-stamp:* ready-made **10** *catch up with sth.:* etwas aufarbeiten **11** *allot sth. to sb.:* give sb. sth. for a particular length of time **16** *calling:* (here) mission **17** *picturesqueness* [ˌpɪktʃəˈresknəs]: (das) Malerische

very short history. It did not begin until the 'sixties, and its Homeric age was over before the century ended. It was created by a passing set of economic circumstances, by cheap open grazing land in the southwest, and good prices on the hoof in Kansas City. It would not survive the invention of barbed-wire. Yet what a legend it has created! Cheap melodrama, whether in fiction, plays or films, soon claimed that legend; yet there always remains a faint gleam of Homeric poetry, not in the monotonous and incredible fables of very good men and very bad men and doll-like heroines, but in the enduring image they give us of a man riding in the wilderness of deserts and mountains, the solitary heroic figure. Here is one who seems to have escaped the economic slavery and universal degradation of our time; who does not compete except with charging animals and the hostile elements; who is seen as the strong free male, careless and smiling and bronzed, the essential male for whom all women have a tenderness. He is a man of our world who has contrived to live his life in an epic simplicity impossible to the rest of us, caught in a bewildering tangle of interests and loyalties.

(From: J. B. Priestley, *Midnight on the Desert*. London: Heinemann Ltd, 1938)

▷ **21** *'sixties:* (here) 1860s **21–22** *Homeric age:* (here) best days **24** *on the hoof:* (of cattle) alive but ready to be killed for food (hence, the need for cowboys to bring the cattle from the plains to the slaughterhouses of Kansas City, etc.) **25** *barbed-wire:* Stacheldraht **36** *contrive to do sth.:* attempt to do sth. **37** *tangle:* confusion

IV. Hollywood

9

Cinema versus Theater

Although Shepard started his career writing for the theatre, he is rare in being one of the few playwrights who has achieved success as a screenplay writer (and as a supporting movie actor).

For a young writer who is seldom given opportunity (and financial assistance) to develop within the nurturing confines of a theatre company, the magnetism of Hollywood exerts a powerful influence. The crossover between stage and screen evinces a rich history in American entertainment. […] In bald mercenary terms, a life in the theatre cannot compete with film and television's financial rewards. It must also be conceded that the status of American theatre appears minuscule in face of film's market size, the expanding reach of global, multimedia corporations, and the movies' impact on cultural consciousness (and consumerism). In the 1993–94 season, a good year for Broadway, attendance of eight million was cause for celebration. Still, the percentage of the U.S. population that attends theatre remains low, suggesting the coterie (or elitist) nature of theatrical performance. Michael Feingold has opined that "to most Americans today a live stage performance is a marginal and exotic phenomenon", and without question the audience drawn by all of American theatre combined, from community playhouses to the Great White

▷ **2** *nurture* (v): feed; support • *confines:* limits **3** *exert influence:* exercise/have influence **4** *evince sth.* (fml): reveal sth., show sth. clearly **5** *bald:* (here) purely • *mercenary* (adj): money, financial **7** *concede sth.:* admit sth. **8** *minuscule* [mɪ'nʌskjuːl]: very small **9** *impact:* effect, influence **10** *consumerism:* belief that spending money on consumer goods is good for the individual and society **11** *attendance:* (here) the number of people attending a performance of sth. **13** *coterie* (adj): of an exclusive circle in society **14** *Michael Feingold:* US theater critic and editor of *Grove's New American Theatre* (1992), from which the quote is taken • *opine* [əʊ'paɪn]: express a certain opinion

Way, cannot measure up the box-office figures generated by any Steven Spielberg or Disney production.

In *True West*, Lee parrots the views of the producer Saul and declares, "In this business we make movies. American movies. Leave the films to the French." (p. 51, ll. 1–2) Lee's pronouncement draws attention to Hollywood's blockbuster mentality and the sensationalist tastes of its audience. It also says something nationalistic about the movies themselves, that the American movie is perhaps the most cherished and dominant art form in American culture. For many theatre artists, this has lead increasingly to the belief that legitimacy only comes when one has "made it" on the screen (and at the box office). Hosts of our country's upcoming writers, even when they pursue work in poetry, fiction, or playwriting, labor in the shadow of the film industry. A writer indifferent to media opportunities faces likely obscurity (and poverty). Success in film or TV not only often serves to consolidate an artist's public reputation, it allows the individual to become involved in one of most influential institutions of the public or private sector – the machine that shapes the very stuff of American dreams. [...] Shepard gained attention as a film actor, in *Days of Heaven* (1978). Since that time Shepard has worked regularly as a screen performer and has amassed a sizable list of credits. [...] The majority of his film roles capitalize on his image as a renegade, the uncompromising nonconformist who eschews convention (and often 'city ways') and retains an inner, private vision.

(From: Leslie A. Wade, *Sam Shepard and the American Theatre, Contributions in Drama and Theatre Studies*, Number 76. Westport: Greenwood Press, 1997)

▷ **17–18** *Great White Way*: nickname for the theater district of Broadway in New York **18** *generate sth.*: bring about sth. **20** *parrot sth.*: repeat sth. which sb. said **26** *cherish sth.*: love and respect sth. **29** *hosts*: large numbers **32** *obscurity:* insignificance, lack of fame **37** *Days of Heaven:* movie about a hot-tempered farm laborer who convinces his girlfriend to marry a rich but dying farmer (played by Sam Shepard) so that they can inherit his belongings **39** *credits:* list of movies in which sb. has appeared • *capitalize on sth.*: take advantage of sth.; profit from sth. **40** *eschew sth.* [ɪs'tʃuː] (fml): avoid sth.

© The Kobal Collection

Sam Shepard was born Samuel Shepard Rogers in Fort Sheridan, Illinois, in 1943. His father was an army pilot, who retired to become a farmer. The family moved around before finally settling in a rural suburb of Los Angeles. As his father was an alcoholic, Shepard's memories of his childhood are not very good. After high school he studied agriculture at college but gave it up to join a touring theatrical troupe who performed plays based on Christian ideas and values.

In 1963 Shepard moved to New York , where he wrote his first two one-act plays *Cowboys* and *The Rock Garden* (1964). Because of their unconventional structure and unusual language, they received mixed reviews. Several other one-act plays followed and some of them won 'Off Broadway' awards ('Obies'). In 1967, his first full-length play, *La Turista*, was performed. In 1979 Shepard won the Pulitzer Prize for his play *Buried Child*, a darkly funny family drama full of powerful and violent metaphors and perhaps Shepard's most chilling analysis of the American family. One year later his play, *True West* (1980) was staged.

Besides being one of America's most important and prolific contemporary playwrights, Sam Shepard is a well-known movie actor and has written the screenplays for many movies, e.g. *Paris, Texas* (1984).

His more than 40 plays deal with modern social concerns, e.g. individual alienation and the destructive forces of family relationships in present-day American society.